The
Successful
Dressage
Competitor

To Karen

Best wishes and

Good luck!

Debby

The
Successful
Dressage
Competitor

Everything you need to know about competing in dressage

DEBBY LUSH

J. A. ALLEN • LONDON

© Debby Lush 2009
First published in Great Britain 2009

ISBN 978 0 85131 962 9

J.A. Allen
Clerkenwell House
Clerkenwell Green
London EC1R 0HT

J.A. Allen is an imprint of Robert Hale Ltd

Photographs by Mick Green and Maggie Wylie except those individually credited on pages 39, 194,
235

British Library Cataloguing in Publication Data
A catalogue record for this book is available from the British Library

Design by Judy Linard
Line illustrations by Carole Vincer, except page 45 which is by Dianne Breeze
Edited by Jane Lake
Printed in China and arranged by New Era Printing Co. Ltd

Contents

Acknowledgements

This book is for Kimberley Battleday, who taught me that there is a lot more to competing than just going to shows!

It is also for my parents who tirelessly carted my various ponies and horses around the countryside to any number and type of competitions, and for Deirdre and Annabel Scrimgeour, who showed me how to do it professionally and who started me off on my judging career by volunteering me to judge a Pony Club Junior Horse Trials walk and trot test.

Many thanks are due to those clients of mine who allowed me to use photographs of them, even when caught in less than flattering moments! And again my gratitude to Mick Green for his patience and dedication to detail in those long photo shoots, and to Maggie Wylie, her sister Mary and husband Ewen, and also Kimberley for being ever ready with their cameras whenever the Scottish weather permitted!

Foreword

Dressage demands high standards of skill, style, physical and mental preparation from both horse and rider. For years experts have written about the art of riding. This makes it difficult to find something new to say, but Debby has, I feel, incorporated a lot of new information about how to be successful – particularly in your attitude to getting the very best from your horse, in presenting tests that will make you proud of your horse and presenting to the judges what they really want to see.

Debby's advice and thoughts are based on valuable experience and I am delighted to recommend it as a 'must-read' to all dressage riders wanting to progress up the ladder. This book will make you want to go out and compete with a far better understanding of your riding – it's inspirational!

CARL HESTER

Introduction

Think back to the last few times you rode in a dressage competition: did you get what you were hoping for from the experience? Were your scores as high as you expected them to be? Did you enjoy competing or did you find it stressful?

Riding to train a horse and riding to compete in dressage tests are two very different skills and you may be better at one than the other; very few people are equally good at both. Perhaps you are happy to remain in the training arena and feel no urge to compete, but for many riders training is the means to produce a horse to a competitive standard, and if this applies to you, you will need to develop and hone *both* skills.

Put simply, the **art of training** involves exposing your horse's weaknesses and then addressing them through education and exercises; the **art of competing** is that of presenting your horse in such a way that any training issues are not obvious to the eye – especially that of the judge! This does not mean that you can neglect training because it is an important factor in your horse's long term well-being as well as your tool for progressing towards higher competitive goals, but merely that to gain the highest marks possible you do not want to make his weaknesses any more apparent in a dressage test than you can help.

Presentation involves such factors as your turnout, the first impression you give the judge and your riding of each movement, turn and transition. It is also, in the eventuality that something goes wrong, about dealing with things calmly and effectively and continuing without allowing anything to adversely affect the remainder of your test.

Competing successfully also depends on a whole range of careful preparations that you need to make before you even go to a show, including choosing when and where to compete, learning and practising tests, having all your equipment organised, and then having a clear routine to follow once you arrive at the show.

Reaching the stage where you can achieve all of these things with ease and confidence is partially down to familiarity: you need to go to shows, make mistakes and learn from them. However, the better prepared you are in terms of knowing what to expect and being ready for it, the less stressful and, hopefully, more enjoyable the experience will become.

The Aim of this Book

This book is designed with specific regard to producing movements in competition dressage tests; all aspects of training and aiding the work involved are covered fully in my previous book, *The Building Blocks of Training* (J. A. Allen, 2008).

Part One

Foundations

1 The Successful Competitor

So what does it take to be a successful competitor? First, let's take a look at what we mean by 'successful'. Does this always equate to 'winning'? It may well, but it can also mean achieving a goal you have set for yourself. This may be as simple as giving your horse a good ride or not coming bottom in a strong class, or it could be achieving or bettering a percentage score. It might simply be to make it all the way through the test without leaving the arena!

You may take your horse to shows simply because you enjoy the social aspect and that's fine, but if you want to be *competitive* during that outing you should try to have clear cut goals in mind before you go.

Aspects of Competition

Start by deciding *why* you want to compete.

Reasons for Competing

There are numerous possible reasons, including:

- Gaining feedback from an unbiased stranger (the judge) on the quality and progression of your training.

- Giving a young or inexperienced horse experience of, and confidence in, the competitive environment.

- Taking part in a social event.

- Attempting to qualify for a Championship.

- Gaining experience at a new level.

- Winning.

- As part of your profession.

- Diagnosing a problem associated with competition that does not occur in training.

- Enjoyment.

Whatever your reason, you have a responsibility to your horse to ensure that he is as adequately prepared, both mentally and physically, as possible before you take him to a show; after all, it is your choice to compete, not his! Without doubt, many horses enjoy competing but only if the foundations are correctly laid for a stress-free experience. Only then will he perform to the best of his ability and enable *you* to enjoy things too.

Are You Ready to Compete?

Consider this question *before* you put that entry in the post, not when you arrive at the show! Again, there are a number of aspects to consider.

- Ideally you and your horse should **be working at least one competitive level above** the one in which you intend to compete. This means that before you compete in Preliminary, you should be tackling Novice level work at home; to compete in Novice you should be training Elementary work at home, and so on up the levels. The reason behind this is that for your horse to find the test work easy (or at least comfortable) within the arena, he should not find it stressful. Any new movements that he is learning, or a new way of going, such as increased engagement, may make him anxious. To enjoy competing and to be successful you need him to be relaxed, and so in competition he should only be asked to perform work with which he is familiar and comfortable. For example, taking a young horse into a Preliminary test when he can barely canter a 20 m circle at home, and asking him to perform a series of movements and transitions in a strange (stressful) environment will not give him a good memory upon which to build a successful, relaxed and enjoyable competition career.

- His **stage of training** should also be taken into account. At certain stages, particularly when learning new and difficult movements, he is likely to be tense even in a training situation. This is not a sensible time to take him out to compete. For example, when he is learning simple changes for the first time he may become quite anxious about transitions into and out of canter; this is not something you can avoid in a test and the extra stress of doing them in competition may cause tension problems in the future.

- Is **your horse fit enough**? To perform a dressage test with ease, your horse needs to be in appropriate condition. Contrary to some people's belief, dressage is a physically demanding sport: horses in so-called 'show condition' carry too much weight for the amount of work involved in a full warm-up and one (or two or even three) tests. His breathing may become laboured (especially in warm weather) and he might struggle to get enough oxygen to his muscles for the work required. Tired muscles are easily damaged and he may become sore and jaded, leaving him with a negative memory of competing.

- Are **you fit enough** to complete a warm-up and your chosen class/es without becoming exhausted? A tired rider will find it hard to maintain posture and have the muscular control to give refined aiding. At worst you may flop in the saddle making for an uncomfortable ride for you both.

- The **time of year** is worth taking into consideration. A sharp horse will be more difficult in the winter, whilst heavier types may find it stressful to compete in hot weather. Of course if you are a serious competitor you will need to be able to cope with all conditions, but if you do it for fun, or you have an inexperienced horse and there is no need to get out there immediately, why put yourself under that unnecessary pressure?

- Are **you confident enough** in your training to display it under a judge's scrutiny? Competing before you are ready and receiving a low score could damage your confidence; you may even feel that you do not want to do it again. Trying to explain to friends and family why your score is so low can also be stressful, especially if they have expectations of you. If you are unsure about being ready, wait a bit longer before putting yourself under pressure. On the other hand, it is also possible to wait too long; competing is one of those skills that can only be honed by getting out there and doing it!

Goal Setting

To get the most out of your competing, try to set yourself goals, both long- and short-term.

Examples of long-term goals would be:

- To affiliate **to your national governing body for dressage** in six months time.

- To compete at a higher level next year.

- To aim for Advanced as an ultimate goal for your partnership.

Short-term goals would be:

- To gain a higher percentage in your next class.

- To achieve at least half your next test in sitting trot.

- To stay inside the arena!

Your goals (especially long-term) will depend on where you are currently with your riding experience, where your horse is, and how far beyond your comfort zone you are willing to push yourself.

Be ambitious with your long-term goals: you might never achieve them, but in striving to reach them you will go far further than if you limit yourself with so-called 'realistic' goals.

Be more cautious with short-term goals. Never set a goal that you are clearly unlikely to achieve. Progress with horses is made in *tiny, incremental pieces*, not huge leaps, and your short-term goals should reflect this, or you will put too much pressure on both of you.

Goal setting gives purpose to your rides. It focuses your mind and will enable you to ride with more concentration and positivity that in turn will give your horse a sense of security. Horses derive confidence from being given clear instructions and, as a result, are more co-operative and willing when ridden in this manner.

If you really want to achieve something (your goal) you will do your best and your results will be better than if you drift along without clear purpose.

If you compete because *you think you ought to*, or because *someone else thinks you ought to*, your heart will not be in it and you will not ride in the same positive, clear manner, which, believe me, your horse *will* pick up and become either nervous (spooky) or lacking in purpose.

Inevitably, you will not achieve all of your goals. Don't be downhearted; when something does not go according to plan (a common occurrence with horses) don't abandon your original goal but make alternative plans instead that lead back towards it. Being flexible in your approach will allow you to overcome setbacks and may even provide you with new horizons or different, even better, goals.

Is Competing Damaging to Your Training?

Almost certainly the answer is 'yes', but the effects will only be severely damaging if one or other of you is unprepared for the experience.

In training, you have the luxury of endless time for preparation – for a transition, for a movement, turn or circle. If things are not exactly how you want them to be, then you will wait until they are; in this way your horse only ever learns to do things right because he is given the maximum preparation before being asked to perform.

In competition, a degree of accuracy is demanded: you must do the transition or movement at a prescribed point in the arena, which restricts preparation time so that you will often need to ask for a response when your horse is *not* perfectly set up for it. As a consequence, he may learn that it is possible to do things wrong, in a slipshod manner, or he might become tense and anxious as he is unable to comply with your demand. As a horse learns from all experiences and his reactions are based on memories, these negative educational experiences will likely transfer back into his training. It is then up to you to correct these issues before you go out to compete again.

In the earlier-level classes, judges expect to see mistakes. It is their job to see the basic training and quality of gaits beneath the errors. The last thing they want to see is a horse so drilled in accuracy that his elastic body has stiffened and his natural flamboyance has been sacrificed to precision, and so always try to ride with his way of going as more of a priority than accuracy.

How Often Should You Compete?

This is again dependant upon a number of factors, the most important being your competing-to-training ratio.

If you visit a lot of local shows, you will undoubtedly see some of the same competitors at every show. These are the riders who compete week in, week out, displaying the same training issues and gaining the same percentages at every outing. They live in hope that their training problems will somehow sort themselves out, or that they might finally find a judge who actually 'likes' their horse.

Sadly neither of these outcomes is likely. Training issues can only be addressed in training sessions, not inside the competition arena, and whilst there may be some variation between judges (see Affiliated or Unaffiliated? on page 33), for the most part judges are trained to look for the same things, and not to 'like' or 'dislike' certain types of horse.

If you are campaigning to qualify for a Championship, or trying to gain points towards a league table, then attending a run of shows with little time between them will not be too detrimental to your training as long as your horse is confident at the level. It is, however, important to consider that competing and travelling are both potentially stressful, as is stabling away at longer shows. A tired horse will be more prone to picking up infections or minor injuries, and a mentally tired horse can become stale resulting in reduced enthusiasm in the arena.

Try to plan your outings well in advance and look carefully at schedules so that you can space competitions logically with time for training interspersed between them. This is likely to vary at different times of year, but forward planning is a great tool in the careful preparation necessary to get the best experience out of each show.

2 Your Mental Approach to Competing

Now that you have considered why, when and how often you might compete, take a moment to think about your *attitude* to competing as this will affect both your mental and physical approaches to test riding, which in turn will affect your horse's responses.

Clearly your attitude will vary somewhat according to your goal for each individual class, but for your horse, *every class is the same*. The environment around the arena will vary and that may affect his confidence and, as a result, his attention to you, but what you ask him to perform within the arena is the same, whether you are going all out to win, or just having fun. *You* are the one who can help him either to feel relaxed, or to feel tense and pressurised.

Assuming that you have taken the care to ensure that his training level is comfortably up to the requirements of your chosen test, then you should set out to **give him the best possible experience that you can.**

The most successful tests (whatever definition of success you are using) are the ones where you are both relaxed and enjoying yourselves and this is most often down to your mental approach to competing.

Positive Mental Attitude

Many different factors go into a successful ride, but if you had to boil them down to the single most important one, it would be positive mental attitude. We've all heard this phrase, sometimes relating to sports, sometimes to careers or just about life in general, and if you want success in any field, developing a positive mental attitude is essential.

If you listen to, or read, interviews with top international competitors after a successful show, you will notice that they almost always say: 'My horse felt really confident today'. At top level where all the riders already have a history of considerable success, the difference on the day is often down to this one small factor: their horse was the most confident in the class.

So what makes a confident horse? A rider who is relaxed and yet positive in her mental approach as she will be able to aid every step of the test with calm clarity. Of course the preparation for the show, and the patient systematic training of the horse throughout his life are also essential, but these are also dependent on the positive approach of the rider.

Developing a Positive Mental Approach

With the possible exception of the professional rider on a mega-expensive purpose-bred super horse who has never been beaten, we all have some confidence issues that we need to control, as opposed to allowing them to control us. You can't just 'pull yourself together' and 'have confidence'; there are a number of factors to recognise, accept and learn how to manipulate to your advantage, but it *can* be done.

State of Mind

Think back to a recent competition and recall your **state of mind**. Was it positive, or was it negative? Did you believe you could win, or were you convinced that you were doomed to failure? How did you finish that competition? Were your expectations/fears confirmed?

It can be very comforting to expect the worst because, whatever happens, you are never disappointed, and sometimes you are pleasantly surprised when things do not go as badly as expected. This is, however, a self-limiting approach: no matter how pleasantly surprised you may be, you will never do your best if this is your approach because your focus will not be on riding as positively as you are able, to produce the best ride of which you are capable.

Imagining the worst and *preparing for* the worst are two totally different approaches. The human mind is wired up to produce whatever you focus on. If, for example, you focus on that scary bunch of flowers waving in the breeze beside the E marker, your body will tell your horse: 'look, there's something to be frightened of!' Result: he spooks at the flowers.

Alternatively, you can notice the potential problem, and plan how to avoid it by concentrating on keeping him focused on the inside of the arena as you pass E, perhaps with a little extra flexion to the inside, a slight shoulder-fore or, in extreme situations, a shoulder-in. In both cases you have noticed the same potential problem but your mental approach to dealing with it was quite different.

You can alter your state of mind rather than being a victim of it. You have two possible tactics for how to do this: just pick the one that you find the easiest.

1. Visualisation. Picture in your mind someone riding how you've always wanted to ride. It might be someone you know, your trainer, a fellow competitor, or a top rider at the Olympics. Now in your mind picture yourself riding like that,

it might be a whole test, or just a snapshot moment; it doesn't matter, the important thing is to mentally see yourself riding like that. Psychologists have proven that the human nervous system does not differentiate between an actual experience and one that is vividly imagined, you will, therefore, find your mind recreating what you see in your imagination, and your body taking on the characteristics of the ride that you are picturing. This means that you can improve your performance with virtual practice! Added advantages to practising in your imagination are lack of pressure, and that whilst inside your mind you will always get it right! Next time you enter a warm-up area, and also as you ride from the warm-up area to the competition arena, recall your inspirational rider and let your mind do the rest.

2. Recreate feelings. Every time you get a good feeling whilst riding – it might be a fantastic canter strike-off, or a super 10 m circle – take the time to replay that feeling in your mind after you finish riding. It might even be the feeling of that glow of pleasure when your trainer compliments you on a particular exercise. Whatever it is that created that good feeling, keep replaying it mentally every so often for the rest of the day and just before you go to sleep. If you can do so, continue to replay the feeling for a few days after the experience (or until you have another great feeling to memorise) and certainly as you start each ride. That feeling, however brief, will suffuse you with a feeling of self-confidence and self-belief that actually you *can* do this, and if you recreate the feeling when you ride at a show, you will create within you the *positive* state of mind that you need to ride at your peak ability.

Concentration

What do you concentrate on when riding at a show? Stress and pressure can easily cause you to become distracted by thoughts that are irrelevant to your performance: how nervous you feel, are you really up to riding this test, what are your chances against the opposition, is your horse going to shy? You are certainly concentrating, but not on your horse!

Try to refine your attention span: if you are noticing things outside the arena, the span is too wide; if you are focussing just on how you feel, it is too narrow. Learn to recognise distracting thoughts and find a way to block them out. There are several mental techniques to do just this, ranging from mentally drawing a big red X through them, to surrounding yourself with a bubble that keeps them out.

Make a point also of *not* concentrating on the outcome. Have you stood at the scoreboard before the class and thought 'I've beaten all of these people before so I should be able to win today', only to end up in the bottom half of the class? Or looked at the names on the board and decided that you don't stand a chance, only to do fairly well? Concentrating on winning will make you overanxious and likely to make mistakes or communicate nervousness to your horse. There is nothing you can do to control the results, so just forget about them and focus on the harmonious relationship with your horse that produces the best results.

Self-doubt and 'Loser's Limp'

Quite reasonably, your conscious mind will ask valid questions such as:

- Why do I think I can do this when I'm an amateur riding against professionals?
- How can I seriously expect to compete against all these big-moving Warmbloods when I am riding a Thoroughbred?

You may also be a victim of 'loser's limp', with realistic reasons for why your success is limited, such as:

- I don't have the money/time/physical shape to do this sport properly.
- I started riding too late in life.
- I broke my left leg five years ago, and it has less strength than the other one.

With these 'reasons' you take the pressure off by giving yourself permission to ride at less than your best; they are also the reasons *why* you do not ride as well as you might, as your mind willingly cooperates with you to create the lack of results that you expect. Throughout the sport of dressage you will find people who have succeeded against all odds – lack of money, difficult physical shapes, even physical disabilities. Try watching a Para Equestrian competition and then see if you still feel the same about your 'problem'.

If you doubt yourself, your horse will have no belief in you either.

Self-image and Self-belief

Self-image plays a big factor in the way that you perform, and make no mistake: *competing is about performing.* However you conceive yourself to *be* will dictate your actions, feelings and behaviour. Despite all conscious efforts to do otherwise, these aspects are under subconscious control, not conscious, and you literally cannot act otherwise, so you need to strive to cultivate a positive self-image. This applies to *your whole life*, not just to your riding career, as the one is impossible to isolate from the other. Negative thinking in life is catching and will only drag you down and keep you there; try to be around positive, enthusiastic people and limit your exposure to those whose only outlook is negative. If this means, for example, moving to a different stable yard, so be it. You will both enjoy your competing more and be more successful when your entire outlook is more positive.

Also, take time to think carefully about your beliefs regarding your riding ability; they may be right or wrong but, even if wrong, your mind will act as if they are right. For example, if you believe 'I can't do sitting trot', you won't ever be able to do it. No matter how hard you try in your lessons, and how you listen to your instructor trying to help you to achieve a sitting-trot seat, because your mind believes that you 'can't do it', it will command your body to defeat your conscious efforts, so fulfilling your belief. Your body will fail to achieve the necessary muscle tone and your stomach muscles will not coordinate the alternating contraction/relaxation pulses needed to swing your pelvis in harmony with your horse's back. And all because *you* have told your body that it is impossible!

Try instead to reframe such beliefs as *challenges*: 'I find sitting trot difficult but I am learning how to do it'.

Positive Framing

In the same way that your mind will action what you *think*, it will also action what you *say*. Once you verbalise a thought, it is recorded in your mind. For instance, if you say: 'I get really nervous as soon as I go to the competition arena', that is what will happen. If, on the other hand, you reframe this into a positive action and say *out loud*: 'I can't wait to get to the competition arena – that's when I really start to enjoy things,' you can talk yourself into believing that what you say is what you will experience.

Try making such positive statements aloud to other people, and to yourself; as your mind starts to action your words you will find that it is true – you *do* enjoy competing!

Think about the words you use and try to always frame things in a positive fashion. One of the most limiting words in existence is 'can't'. Try to lose it from your vocabulary. Just because you haven't managed something before, don't exclude yourself from ever being able to do it by telling your mind that you can't; your mind will be only too happy to comply with you by refusing to enable whatever action it is.

Also, try not to call something a *problem;* rename it a *challenge*. Challenges can be tackled and are an opportunity to become a better rider; problems are sometimes too tough to be faced. Likewise, try to replace 'if' with 'when'. 'If' gives you a feeling of self-doubt. 'If I could sit the trot', should become 'When I can sit the trot'.

As Jane Savoie says in *That Winning Feeling* (J.A.Allen, 1992): 'The victim complains and feels overwhelmed. The winner knows he can't alter the facts, but he can always decide how he'll react to those facts and what he'll say. Victim or victor. It's your choice.'

Dealing with Competition Nerves

Even the most successful competitor will experience a form of competition nerves, but these superstars of the equestrian world have learned, or in some cases have a natural mental makeup that allows them, to *use* the adrenalin that creates nerves to produce a higher level of performance, with increased alertness and focus *on their horse.*

If you suffer from competition nerves, take the time to notice that when you are feeling nervous your mind is anywhere *but* on your horse. You may be worrying about how he will behave, with your attention on the external things (flower pots, other horses, atmosphere) that might cause him to misbehave, not actually on *him.*

Studies of horses in their natural environment have shown that the social order within the wild herd is dependent upon the *attention* that individuals accord one another. Horses derive a sense of security from being in a clear social position within any relationship, and so any sudden changes in the normal mutual attention levels between you will cause him to become anxious, with anxiety resulting in altered behaviour patterns.

He should be used to your undivided attention when schooling at home, and so this is what you should strive to give him when you are competing. In other words: **Ride your horse, not the test.** This is obviously easier said than done but there are many ways of training yourself to do this, and you *can* train yourself to do this, rather than be a victim of your nerves forever.

- All the subjects covered in this section have a place in this: they are all important to your ability to channel that nervous adrenalin into positive action.

- You may find that now you understand a little more about the effect you are having on your horse, you will be able to go into a competition environment focused on giving *him* as much help, i.e. attention, as you can, and this will be enough to bring your nerves under control and improve your performances.

- You could try a deliberate effort to *change* your state of mind using one of the techniques described above. Remember that your mind will strive to create what you are imaging – great feelings or picturing yourself riding like your idol; either one of these will endow you with the confidence that you *can* do this, and whilst your mind is occupied with this task, it will be too busy to worry!

- Try a bit of acting. Pretend that you are supremely confident, and that you are really looking forward to getting inside that arena to show everyone what you can do. Talk about it aloud – you will be amazed what you can talk yourself into! Not only will you present a confident exterior, your mind will take on that mantle and *believe* it. Take care not to tell yourself (or anybody else) how nervous you are going to be, or you will believe that instead. Act confidently and positively: action leaves no time to dwell on fear.

- If your nerves are about losing, or showing yourself up, you need to realise that *action cures fear; inaction breeds fear.* The more you are indecisive, the greater the problem becomes. *Take a risk.* If something doesn't come off, it's not a disaster – treat it as a great opportunity to learn – next time you will be prepared for it.

- You may need help from a coach or a sports psychologist to identify your own individual trigger points for nervousness. Don't be shy to ask for help. Remember: you can *learn* to control your nerves.

- Remember to **smile**! Smiling relaxes over 100 muscles in and around your face – it's hard to hold onto negative thoughts when you smile.

For more in-depth reading on the topics covered above, see: *That Winning Feeling* by Jane Savoie (J. A. Allen 1992) and *Score More for Dressage* by Wendy Jago (J. A. Allen 2006).

Learning from Your Mistakes

You will make mistakes. We all do, unavoidably. The important thing to *do* about these mistakes is to learn from them, and not to make the same errors again.

We have looked already at developing a positive mental approach and the way this can affect performance. On the other hand, if you *are* a confident rider you can also make errors by putting either yourself or your horse under too much pressure to perform. This might be in an effort to win an important class, or because you feel under pressure from other people (relatives, owners etc.) to produce a good performance, or simply because you really want to do your best. Whatever the reason, you may cause undue tension in your horse by asking for just that bit too much for his level of physical or mental competence *at this time.*

Be honest enough in your assessment afterward to recognise that you made the error, not him. That way you will be more conscious of exactly what demands you are putting on him next time. Certainly, if you are both feeling on top form when you begin your test you should ask for all he can give, but take care never to ask for more than he is comfortable with at his current stage of training.

3 Choose Your Competitions

Test Considerations

At What Level Should You Compete?

I mentioned in Chapter 1 the ideal of always competing at a level below the one at which you are training and why this is necessary for your horse's confidence. With the advent of Introductory tests that include only walk and trot, there is no reason not to adhere to this principle. You may still be *perfecting* certain movements in your competition tests, but nothing you are going to ask him to do in the arena should be new to him.

Choosing Suitable Tests

You may be constrained by circumstances in the tests that you choose to ride in, especially if you are in an area with limited local shows but, if at all possible, read through the tests available and make a choice based on suitability to your individual horse *before* entering a competition.

Take care not to enter classes based just on the *level* of test unless your horse is highly competent at that level and finding all the work easy and, even if he is, some tests will undoubtedly suit him better than others.

Consider Novice-level tests: some include counter-canter, others do not; some include rein-back, others do not; some include walk to canter, others do not. The movements are there to make the judge's job easier by displaying the strengths and weaknesses of your basic training. *Know* those strengths and weaknesses.

Bear in mind that one of your goals in competition should always be to give him the most comfortable ride that you can, without stress, and you will start to pick your tests accordingly.

This is not to say that you should avoid the tests that he finds more difficult indefinitely, but that you should continue to work on his weaker areas until he is competent enough to be put under the pressure of producing them in competition.

If you are just moving up a level, one of the best ways to introduce the new work is to compose a Freestyle test. Although the movements required at each level are set, you are free to position them wherever you choose in the arena, giving you the freedom to design a test that includes all the preparation he needs for the movements that he finds more difficult. (See Chapter 29 for more details on constructing a Freestyle test.)

Understanding the Construction of Dressage Tests

Dressage tests are constructed in a carefully progressive manner, the object being to guide your training in the right direction, and to make movements only progressively more difficult as you move up the competition levels.

As an overview, Preliminary tests are constructed to have easy, flowing lines with no sharp turns, and transitions that are positioned in the easiest places for your horse to perform them. The overall aim of Preliminary tests is to encourage relaxation, rhythm and forward thinking. Transitions are often asked for *between* markers to allow for preparation time, and the circles and half-circles are all large enough that even the less supple horses can manage them with a degree of ease.

Preliminary level is basically concerned with the first two of the Scales of Training:

1.   **Rhythm** (and relaxation), and

2.   **Suppleness,** and touching on the third:

3.   **Contact**.

Novice level tests begin to demand a little more: the transitions happen *at* the marker – and there are many more of them – smaller circles, rein-back, direct *upward* transitions such as walk to canter, short (straight) sections of counter-canter, small amounts of medium trot and medium canter.

Novice level work should consolidate the first two Scales of Training and add the next two:

3.   **Contact** and

4.   **Impulsion**, and touch on the fifth:

5.   **Straightness**.

Elementary tests begin to demand a small degree of collection in the work, just enough to be able to perform the slightly more difficult movements with ease. Leg-yield is introduced, as is the simple change, and rein-back to trot. Counter-canter is asked for on the curve, there are 10 m circles in canter, and medium gaits must be performed from marker to marker with clear transitions at start and finish. Many more changes of bend are demanded as are ever-increasing numbers of transitions, often with individual marks for those transitions.

This level of test should consolidate the first four Scales, and add the last two:

5. **Straightness** and

6. **Collection**.

From Medium level upward the Scales of Training should become increasingly developed. For example the Medium horse will be straighter than the Novice horse, whilst the Grand Prix horse will have a far more clearly defined rhythm than the Preliminary horse.

(For more details on the Scales of Training, see Chapter 31.)

Notice Where Marks are Awarded

Once you have learned the patterns of a test, read the test sheet again and notice how movements are split up for the purpose of awarding marks: you will start to realise that certain tests emphasise certain points. For example, Novice and Elementary tests have far more marks for individual transitions than do Preliminary tests. *The aim is to make you focus on improving your transitions.*

Certain tests have double marks for the walk, or have the walk section split into more than one mark; this should make you take more care of your horse's walk.

Some test sheets include 'directives'. These are designed as guidance to both the judge and the competitor of the priority points that are being judged *within* each movement.

Always remember: it is not just the production of the movement that is being judged but also the *way* that your horse moves whilst doing it, this latter being the most important feature for success.

Progressive Introduction of Movements

As already mentioned, tests are carefully designed to increase in difficulty *gradually*. This not only applies to the inclusion of gradually more demanding movements, but also to *where* those movements are placed within the test.

A good example of this is the simple change. It first appears at Elementary level and is positioned *shortly after a turn*. You may think that this makes it hard but, if ridden with thought, it is actually *easier* for your horse.

A small degree of collection (which is necessary for a good downward transition) is easiest to produce on a correctly ridden curve because your horse's

Leave the arena in walk on a long rein where appropriate

COLLECTIVE MARKS

* 13.   Rhythm, correct footfalls, regularity, suitable and consistent tempo

* 14.   Suppleness: relaxed mentally and physically. Works over back and through neck. Follows line of curves equally to both directions

* 15.   Contact: works from behind into a consistent elastic contact

* 16.   Rider's position: balance, straightness and correctness

* 17.   Rider's results: effectiveness and correctness of aids

Final Mark: 230

All movements will be awarded 10 marks with the exception of * movements which will have

© **Published by British Dressage.** All rights reserved. No part of this Publication to be transmitted in any form or by any means: electronic, mechanical, photocopying, recording of British Dressage.

INTRODUCTORY A
Arena 20m x 40m
Approximate time 4 minutes

2008

BRITISH DRESSAGE

1.	A	Enter in working trot and proceed down the centre line without halting	Straightness on centre line, evenness of contact, quality of turn at C.
	C	Turn right....................	
2.	B	Circle right 20 metres diameter................	Regularity & tempo. Uniform bend along the line of the circle
3.	B	Working trot	
	Between		
	B & F	Transition to walk (3-7 steps) and proceed in working trot	Fluency, clarity of walk, relaxation
4.	E	Half circle right 10 metres diameter to X	Regularity & tempo.
	X	Half circle left 10 metres diameter to B........	Uniform bend along the line of half circles
5.	Between	Transition to walk (3-7 steps) and	
	B & M	proceed in working trot	Fluency, clarity of walk, relaxation
6.	E	Circle left 20 metres diameter	Regularity and tempo. Suppleness and contact. Uniform bend along line of circle
7.	Between		Fluency & throughness of transition.
	K & A	Transition to medium walk................	Regularity & relaxation of walk
* 8.	FXH	Change the rein in a free walk on a long rein................	Regularity, relaxation, purpose, stretching forwards and down, ground cover, suppleness of whole body.
9.	H	Medium walk	
	C	Circle right 20 metres diameter	
	Between		Regularity, purpose, relaxation. Freedom of walk.
	X & C	Transition to working trot................	Fluency & throughness of the transition
10.	MXK	Change rein in working trot	Regularity & tempo, suppleness & contact
11.	A	Down the centre line	Balance in turn, straightness, fluency & throughness of
	X	Medium walk................	transition
12.	G	Halt, immobility, salute	Fluency and throughness of transition. Balance and relaxation in halt.

A British Dressage test sheet with directives. (www.britishdressage.co.uk)

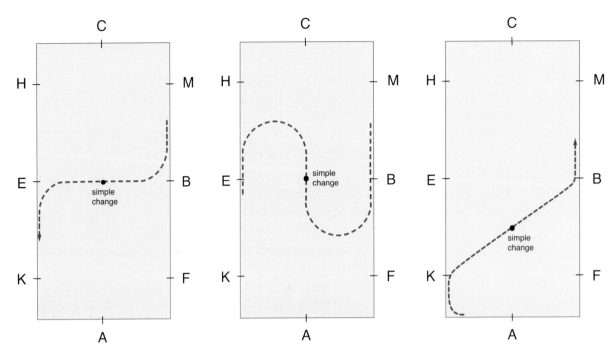

Simple change patterns at elementary level, each with a short turn before the downward transition to assist with collection and balance immediately prior to the transition. (*Left*) Simple change across the half school (E–B) line, (*centre*) in the middle of two half 10 m circles, and (*right*) across the short diagonal.

inside hind leg is further forward beneath his body during bending. The tighter the curve (and so the greater the bend) the more engaged the hind leg, resulting in the hind leg supporting an increased percentage of his body-weight, i.e. collection. This makes the first few steps out of any turn the most collected that you can achieve for his stage of training and so the best place in which to make a direct downward transition. At this level, the downward transition is permitted to be not quite direct, and so a step or two of trot before he walks can still gain a reasonable mark.

In the next level up, Medium, simple changes are required in the centre (over X) of the long diagonal, where you have no preparatory assistance from the pattern. You must be able to produce collection purely from your half-halts, and unless the downward transition is clearly direct, i.e. no trot steps at all, your mark will be low.

Arena Size

As in all things to do with competing, you will at some point need to tackle most variables, arena size being one, but as certain horses find one or other size of arena easier, it is only sensible in the early days (either of his competition career as a whole, or at a new level) to choose your tests with the goal of making the experience as positive as possible for him.

Large horses need more space. This might seem blindingly obvious, but then why do so many people insist on competing their big, young, unbalanced horses in small-arena tests?

As always, there is the practical aspect: a venue may only have a small arena, or you may go to a show that has one arena of each size and wish to compete in two classes on the same day. However, *for the best possible experience for your horse –* which is, after all, what we should want, both in terms of building his confidence and for enabling his best performance – try to pick your arenas appropriately. Your long-term results will be better for this selectivity.

Size isn't everything! Some horses become more unbalanced when asked to perform long straight lines and, regardless of their physical size, may find the smaller arena easier, with more frequent corners to aid re-balancing. Smaller-moving horses tend to find the smaller arena easier, especially with respect to producing medium gaits where even the diagonals of the arena are not too long. Some ponies find the large arena quite daunting in terms of the fitness required to travel the extra distance compared to a short-arena test. Big-moving horses may find everything in a small arena test far too close together, and become stressed as a result.

The important thing is to think carefully about your own individual horse and, possibly with advice from your trainer or an experienced friend, pick competitions in the appropriate arena size until he is more capable of coping with either.

Once again: **read the test before you put in your entry!**

Affiliated or Unaffiliated?

Deciding whether, or when, to affiliate is dependent upon a number of considerations.

- Cost. Clearly, unaffiliated shows are cheaper to attend than affiliated. If you affiliate you not only have annual membership fees to pay, but also annual registration fees for each horse and, in general, higher entry fees than at unaffiliated shows. You may also find that travelling costs to unaffiliated shows are less, as venues may be more local.

- Do you feel good enough? You may feel that either you or your horse is not up to standard for affiliated competition. If this is your belief, even if you do take the plunge and affiliate, you will probably prove yourself right by riding with a lack of self-confidence (see previous chapter) and so produce poor performances. On the other hand, you may be correct in your belief – at this moment. This is a good time to ask the advice of a trainer or judge who can advise you either to wait and further your training before affiliating, or tell you to 'get on with it'.

- Class tickets (available from British Dressage) are a good way of dipping your toe in the water as they allow you to enter affiliated classes without having the expense of affiliating. You will not be eligible to win points or qualify for championships, but they can be a good way of trying out the system and seeing if it is for you.

- Anxiety about competing against professionals or very experienced riders can be off-putting but, initially at least, you will be able to ride in the Restricted sections of classes. This means that although you may ride in the same class as the professionals and be judged against them on the scoreboard, your final placing will be relative to other Restricted riders as opposed to the experienced and professional riders who must ride in the Open sections. See the current British Dressage (BD) rule book for definitions of Open and Restricted riders, but in brief it means that Restricted competitors are those who have no real experience of competing at higher levels. They may have *attempted* a test or two at the next level up, but are not yet experienced at that higher level. As a result, you can be assured that you are competing against other riders who have similar experience to yourself.

- Standard of judges. Anyone can judge an unaffiliated class, so you may get some very varied results and comments. Affiliated judges, on the other hand, go through extensive training and examination systems, with compulsory on-going training required to maintain their status on the lists. Whilst you will always get some individual variation between judges, all those on the affiliated lists will be judging you with an educated eye, and a clear understanding of the correct training required to progress. You can by no means be assured of this at unaffiliated shows.

- Standard of facilities. Affiliated showgrounds are required to provide minimum standards of facilities, particularly with respect to both competition and warm-up arenas, and must state in the schedule if a competition is to be run on a grass arena. Some variations in standards still exist, especially in areas of the country where there are limited venues, but they are all under constant review by British Dressage officials ensuring as high a standard as possible within practical limits. Whilst many venues hold both affiliated and unaffiliated shows, and there are very many unaffiliated shows that have excellent facilities, there is no governing body to ensure the standard of facilities at such shows.

- Rules. Affiliated shows run under British Dressage rules as do British Riding Clubs competitions. Unaffiliated shows *may* run under a specific set of rules but there is no absolute requirement for them to do so. One area where competitors may notice this is in adherence to the size of warm-up arena relative to the number of competition arenas. British Dressage stipulates a minimum size according to the number of arenas running; unaffiliated shows often have no ruling on this, and as a consequence warm-up arenas may become very crowded and not always the safest place to be.

- Insurance. All affiliated shows are covered by British Dressage insurance, whereas unaffiliated shows may not have the same, or indeed any, comprehensive cover. Also, as a benefit of BD membership, you automatically receive Personal Liability and Personal Accident Insurance.

- A lot of unaffiliated venues offer championship series, often with attractive prizes.

- British Dressage offers a comprehensive championship structure, with Area Festival Championships and a Festival Final for the less experienced combinations and, for the more ambitious, summer and winter Regional Championships leading to Winter and National Championships, with classes held at all levels (below Advanced), for both Restricted and Open competitors. All of these championship classes are judged by a panel of judges (two, three or five depending on the class) and so you receive several score sheets for the one test, giving you a lot of feedback. These shows also give you the opportunity to compete in a 'big atmosphere', complete with an audience and prize-givings.

- A limited number of unaffiliated venues and some Riding Clubs offer Freestyle to Music classes. These classes are a great way to have competitive fun, but putting together a programme and music takes time and money, and to get the most use from your efforts you may want to consider competing affiliated, where qualifiers and championships are more readily available at all levels.

British Dressage membership also offers:

- Dedicated young-horse classes.

- A bi-monthly magazine containing all the schedules for the next two months, plus articles on training and related subjects, regional training opportunities with an inter-regional adult team championship, social events and unmounted workshops, plus a training camp and a home international competition (i.e. a competition between teams from England, Scotland, Wales and Northern Ireland using earlier-level classes with riders who are eligible to compete at the appropriate levels).

- Comprehensive training and competition opportunities for under-25s.

● The opportunity to train to become a judge, including organised trips abroad to international shows with a high-listed judge to give you a deeper insight into what you are watching.

Winning Points

Assuming that you have decided to affiliate, you now become eligible to win points. Points are allocated according to your percentage score in classes from Novice level upward. The number of points that *your horse* has gained determines in which levels of competition he is allowed to compete; the level at which *you* gain points determines your rider grouping, which in turn determines whether you must ride in Open or Restricted classes – see the latest British Dressage rule book for details.

Winning your first few points is cause for celebration. However, once you start winning them on a regular basis, you might want to take a moment to consider: are you ready to move up a level? It is all too easy to rush ahead in the quest to gain points, and then find that you have put yourself up into the next level of competition before you are really ready for it.

Points are only gained when you can achieve 60 per cent or more in an affiliated competition. In theory, once you can achieve this sort of percentage on a regular basis, you should be ready to think about moving up to the next level. In reality, there is likely to be a lot more that you still need to achieve in both training and in competition experience before you are really ready to move on up. Probably scores above 65 per cent on a regular basis are more realistic as a guide to your readiness to try another level.

So try to think ahead, especially if your points are nearing the maximum allowed for a certain level, and plan your shows carefully, or you may find yourself ineligible for a championship qualification at a level where you might be successful, and find instead that you are at the next level up before you are ready, and feeling like you are starting at the bottom of the heap once more.

Riding Hors Concours (HC)

Riding Hors Concours means that you can take part in a class for which you are not necessarily eligible, or practise a test without the risk of gaining unwanted points.

You will not be eligible for any prizes or points, nor will your score be put onto the scoreboard, but you will still receive your judging sheet and the important feedback from the judge on your performance.

You cannot declare HC *after* you have ridden.

Bear in mind that organisers are not required to take an HC entry, but unless a class is particularly full, they probably will. See the British Dressage rule book for full details.

4 Foundation Preparations

Foundation preparations are all the things you need to do (as well as the necessary training) before you get anywhere near a competition. They are most relevant to a young horse who has not yet been to a show under saddle, but are equally well worth checking out with a new horse that has an unknown history.

Environment

- Working your horse in company.

- Working him in all weather conditions and at all times of day.

- Getting him used to travelling and standing in the lorry/trailer for long periods.

- Familiarising him with the idea of going away from home to work in different arenas, both alone and with strange horses.

- Staying away from home in strange stables.

- Teaching him to work with distractions, such as people moving around beside the arena whilst he works.

- Habituate him to coming back to work without argument after a short rest break.

- Introducing a car at the end of the arena.

- Introducing him to arena boards, pots of flowers and flags.

- Introducing him to music playing while he works – especially if you intend to have a go at Freestyle competitions.

- Getting him used to applause – you may be in a prize-giving line up one day!

Work through this list in roughly this order to establish your controls before you tackle the more challenging introductions of the real competition environment.

Working in Company

Although you will be alone in the competition arena, the warm-up arena may be a crowded place with lots of horses together, not all of them behaving themselves. If you introduce your horse to working with others at home, where he is in familiar surroundings and feeling confident, he will be less shocked by the warm-up environment when he first encounters it.

Start by introducing one other horse. If necessary to begin with you may even keep them at opposite ends of the arena until they ignore each other. Then try riding past each other. As this is a controlled situation you can ensure that there is plenty of room between you when you first pass whilst travelling in opposite directions. Some horses develop an aversion to other horses coming towards them, which can be quite a problem in the warm-up arena at shows, but if you start in this carefully controlled manner you minimise the risk of this developing.

Gradually have the other horse pass by closer and then start to introduce more than one horse. If this is not possible at home you may need to combine this with trips out to other people's schools (see below), but home is best, so try inviting some riding friends to join you in schooling sessions.

Working in All Weathers

Whilst riding in the wind and rain might not be pleasant, you don't get to choose the weather conditions for a show. Of course you may make the choice to withdraw from a class if the weather is particularly foul but in many circumstances you will find yourself riding in conditions that you would not consider riding in at home.

Make a point of schooling occasionally in bad weather. If your horse is particularly difficult, start by lungeing him in poor conditions, so that he gets the idea that he must work as you want him to no matter what. At the end of the day though, there is no substitute for actually riding in bad conditions and insisting on his cooperation. The more you focus on working him hard, the less you will think about how nasty the weather is, the better you will both focus on his way of going, and not just on surviving the experience! This way, when the weather lets you down at a show, you will both have an established way of dealing with it.

Working at All Times of Day

If you have a horse who works daily to a set routine, you may find him less than cooperative when your class is at seven at night! Shows often run over very extended timetables and you could find yourself competing at any time from well before breakfast to well after teatime.

Make a point of schooling at different times of day, not all the time, but often

The author with Holme Grove Merlin competing in a hailstorm. Both horse and rider are fully focussed on their performance.

Photograph by Kevin Sparrow.

enough that you can notice if he is particularly grumpy when, say, he thinks he should be eating his tea. If you do identify a particular time slot he dislikes, try riding deliberately at that time of day for a while until he accepts that this is going to happen, and that getting grumpy isn't going to get him anywhere.

Travelling and Standing in the Lorry/Trailer

Clearly if you are going to compete, you will need to travel him in either a lorry or a trailer. As some horses find this stressful you should try to accustom him initially to loading and travelling without the added stress of a show on the same day. Of course if he has been shown in-hand as a youngster you will have a head start and may be able to miss out a few of the steps suggested below.

If he enjoys hacking, try to find somewhere safe where you can park and unload, then drive him there and go for a hack. At first, this might even involve hacking home, so that the journey is just one way. This will make the whole experience less stressful, hopefully more enjoyable, and he should become calm about the whole idea of travelling.

If he is not a good hack, then take him to other yards where you can use the school. This might be a friend's yard, or somewhere that you can hire the school, or you might go for a lesson. He might be fine the first time you do this, or it may take a few sessions, but once he is relatively calm when you arrive, start to leave him standing on board for increasing periods before unloading. Do the same after you have ridden him until he stands calmly on board for as long as you want, both before and after work. Having a horse you cannot leave on board your transport at a show is problematic, potentially dangerous, and very tiring!

Riding in Other People's Schools

One of the greatest challenges of competing is being able to produce the same work in the competition arena that you do at home. Work towards this by taking him to unfamiliar arenas where you can ride him for as long as you want until he is settled. You may find that he is best alone or he may be happier in company, and so if you can liaise with a friend who has an arena you can use, you can try both situations and discover which suits him best.

Obviously when he reaches a show, he will need to work in the competition arena on his own, but taking steps early on to make him feel confident in an alien environment is part of the process towards developing a confident competitor.

As suggested already, when he is happy in the strange arena, start to work with other (unfamiliar) horses as well, to accustom him to this situation before putting him in the rather uncontrolled environment of a show warm-up arena.

Find both indoor and outdoor arenas to use, and take him to several different places, not just to one. The extra effort will be worth it in the long run when you take him to a show and he is not intimidated by his surroundings.

Stabling Away

You may well find that at some point you want to stay away at a show, and this can be quite stressful if he has never been away from home before. Start by borrowing a stable to stand him in when you go to other yards to use the school, just for an hour or two, and repeat the exercise on a few separate trips. This will give him the idea that he is not being abandoned somewhere strange.

After this, if you can stable him away from home overnight, maybe at a friend's, or your trainer's, yard, he will not take it badly when you put him in a temporary stable at a show. If you set this pattern early enough in his career, it is not something that needs repeating often, and is certainly worth the effort. A stressed horse in temporary stabling is worrying and tiring for all concerned, including the other horses stabled around him, and their owners.

Distractions

You can often see competitors at shows becoming quite upset with people moving around near the arena because their horses have ceased to pay attention to them, and are looking (or spooking) instead, at the distraction.

One of the main principles of dressage is that of submission, and this is largely defined by how well the horse pays attention to his rider. If you look at the wording of the collective mark for submission at the end of a test sheet, you will see that 'attention' is the first defining word.

Once again, if you accustom him to giving you his full attention in an environment where he is already confident, probably at home, or if that is not practical then in the school of a friend or a trainer, you will have a positive grounding upon which to build. Ask for distractions to be introduced: people walking around outside or inside the arena, pushing wheelbarrows past, playing with dogs, shutting doors nearby – anything you can think of that might take his attention away from you. If he is startled or becomes distracted, insist that he returns his attention to you as quickly as possible and then praise him. This builds the good habit you will want in the arena.

In other words, once you are past the most basic of stages and you have a degree of control, *do not* avoid distractions by being over-controlling of his environment. You will never be in control of his surroundings at a show, so both of you might just as well learn how to get on with things no matter what is happening around you.

Picking Up After a Rest Period

When you work him at home make a habit of taking a number of walk breaks during your schooling. Many horses think that once the reins have been dropped, that signals the end of the session and can be quite awkward and resentful of being gathered up and asked to work again.

One of the challenges of competing is to time your warm-up so precisely that you can go from warm-up arena to competition arena at the ideal moment. There are many factors (weather, nervous tension etc.) that can affect how long your warm-up will take, and even if you get it right you have no guarantee that the *class* will run to time! Being able to stretch your horse out for a break, and then gather him together again smoothly and without resistance will allow you to accommodate such unforeseeable issues without loss of performance, so develop this habit at home.

Cars

Horses become quite used to working in arenas, but introduce a car at the end of it (or even a strange-looking judge's box) and they can become quite rattled. Even the difference between a car and a big four-wheel drive vehicle can be enough to spook them, so try to introduce them to the idea by parking a vehicle at the end of your arena (or even inside it) and ride past it at a safe distance. The more different vehicles you can get him accustomed to, the better.

Arena Boards, Pots of Flowers and Flags

One of the biggest issues for many horses is the waving leaves or flowers of those 'dangerous' plants that organisers like to ambush you with on either side of the A marker, or even at every marker!

Investing in a few flowerpots (preferably tall ones) and putting a few flowering plants, or even plastic plants in them, is well worth the effort. Stand them around inside your arena and leave them for several schooling sessions. Once he ignores them, then move them to a new location and repeat the process.

White arena boards can be another source of spooky behaviour. If you do not want to pay out for actual arena boards, you can use lengths of white plastic guttering as a substitute. This is quite cheap and absolutely safe, and an excellent way of introducing arena boarding. You can also use white-painted trotting poles, but bear in mind that these can roll, and are more likely to trip him up if he steps on them.

If your own school is the same size as a competition arena it is likely that you may never practise with boards. When you first have to ride in a boarded arena, therefore, you may find that not only can these boards be spooky, but also that you and your horse are so used to using the fences of your arena to push you around the turns, you will both feel rather wobbly trying to stay within little boards of fetlock height! For practice, put boards a metre or so inside your own arena fences and ride in a smaller area for a while.

Flags are more difficult to arrange, but it is worth trying to get hold of some. Many venues, especially those that run championships, have flags flying near the arena, with ropes that click against the poles and flags that snap in the wind – altogether disturbing for many horses.

Music

Whilst most horses actually *like* working with music, it is a good idea to at least introduce it to your horse before going to a show, where music may suddenly erupt from a loudspeaker and upset him.

A portable 'boom-box' placed on the arena fence, or on a stand in the corner (somewhere where it is definitely *not* going to fall over) is quite sufficient for the job, and all you need to do is to keep riding past it as if it is not there. This will give him the message that it is not something to pay any attention to.

Applause

Not knowing how your horse will react the first time that he hears applause can make prize-givings an anxious rather than an enjoyable time, and so it is advisable to accustom him to it early.

If you can round up a friend or two at the end of a schooling session, or take the opportunity if anyone comes to watch your lesson, ask them to clap: softly at first and then louder if he is calm. Make sure that he is facing them at first – the sound of clapping coming from behind is often more likely to result in an explosive reaction!

If you get a chance to ride as a guinea-pig at a demonstration, do so, and ask for a round of applause at the end if it is not offered – take every opportunity to expose him to clapping when he is young and in controlled surroundings – again, it will prove well worth the effort for later in life. After all, you never know when you will find yourself in a mounted prize-giving, and assuming that you will do so is in keeping with that positive mental attitude that you are trying to cultivate.

Choosing Your Tack

Along with all the things you need to familiarise your horse with, you will need to establish exactly what tack you will use for competing. Again, certain items are covered by rules. *With saddles, you have no choice*: only the use of English-style saddles is permitted. *With bridles, bits, nosebands, breastplates, balance straps etc., you do have a choice.* **BUT: you still have to stay within the rules, which may change even within a year, so make sure you keep up-to-date with the current rules.**

Bridles

Plain or fancy; fashions come and go: plain, white or coloured padding on browbands and nosebands, clincher browbands, brass buckles and/or keepers, a touch of 'bling' with decorative crystals etc. Sometimes dressing up a horse who has no white on his face can make a more attractive picture, but it is also possible to go over the top; choose wisely.

Bits

You must choose a bit that is not only of an allowed type (see descriptions and diagrams in your rule book) and material, but also of permitted dimensions in terms of the thickness of the mouthpiece, diameter of the rings, and length of the shank with curb bits.

If you have a horse who is difficult to bit, bear in mind what is allowed in competition when you choose a bit for training; there is little point in training him in a bit that is not permitted for competition. There is an ever-increasing range of permitted bits, so try to accustom him from the start to working in one that you will also be able to use when competing.

Snaffle or double bridle?

This choice obviously only applies at a level where double bridles are permitted: check your rule book. If you are intending to compete at a level where you can make this choice, a good idea to start with is to consider *why* you might want to use a double.

If he goes kindly in a snaffle, why put him in a double? Unless you intend to ride in a competition where a double bridle is compulsory, there is no necessity to use one; many horses find two bits in their mouth difficult to accept. On the other hand, some horses seem to *prefer* the double, especially those who favour a straight-bar bit, and some accept the contact more readily in a double than a snaffle: these are legitimate reasons for using one.

What is not acceptable, however, is to use a double bridle to coerce a horse into an 'outline' because you cannot get him there in a snaffle. This is too commonly seen by judges, and cannot be mistaken for anything else as this horse will open his mouth, draw his tongue up, and be tense throughout his frame. Do not think you will fool the judge into believing that you are doing anything but winching his head into place with the bits – you won't.

Nosebands

Once again, rules must be checked as all equestrian sports/events that involve dressage vary on permitted nosebands.

A plain cavesson noseband, not done up so tightly that it needs padding beneath the chin to prevent it from chafing, is the best choice, showing that your horse accepts the contact with a soft, relaxed jaw.

If you need assistance in this department, perhaps with a less educated horse, or one that you are re-schooling, take into account the shape of his head when you choose your noseband. A drop noseband provides less clutter than a Flash on a small head, but can make a long head look even longer. Clearly you should base

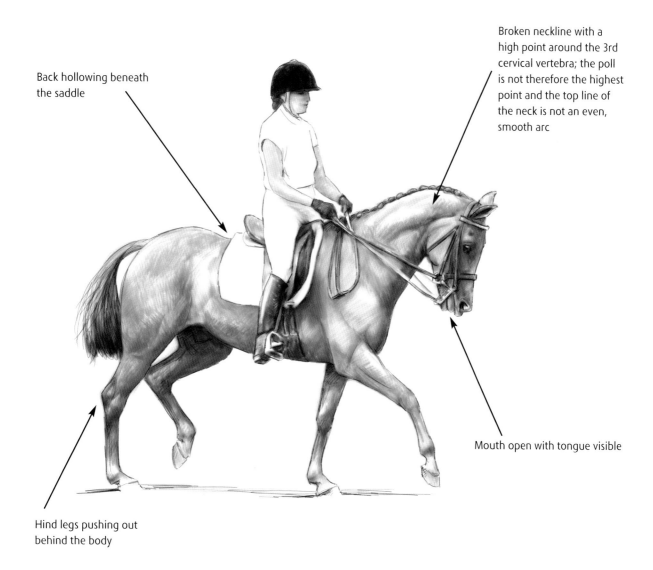

Back hollowing beneath the saddle

Broken neckline with a high point around the 3rd cervical vertebra; the poll is not therefore the highest point and the top line of the neck is not an even, smooth arc

Mouth open with tongue visible

Hind legs pushing out behind the body

This horse's outline does not appear too incorrect at a quick glance, but if you look carefully all the signs of non-acceptance of the bridle are visible.

your choice on the one that you find most effective for your individual horse, but aesthetics are worth taking into account if you can do so.

Whatever your choice, no noseband should ever be closed so tightly as to cause discomfort. Again, it is not something with which you can fool a judge – bulging skin around the noseband and quantities of padding are pretty obvious and do nothing to make the judge happy about a horse's acceptance of the contact. If this is a big problem, you need to address it in training, not just cover it up.

Breastplates

Most people only consider a breastplate if they have a herring-gutted horse who needs it to stop the saddle from slipping backward. Breastplates do, however, have another very useful application: as a neckstrap!

Under British Dressage rules you are not permitted to use a neckstrap in most classes; if you feel in need of one for security, a breastplate is a very suitable alternative.

Balancing Straps

These are permitted under most rules and can be used as discreet assistance for keeping your hands still (for example, in transitions) or helping you to sit the trot on a very bouncy horse. The balancing strap is another alternative to the neck strap, and clutters the horse less, but is not always as secure as the breastplate because it is situated higher up, and is thus less help at anchoring you down in the event of potential flying lessons!

A balancing strap attached to the front of the saddle.

Saddles

Whilst a dressage saddle is ideal, because it is designed to place you in the most effective position for flat work, it is not absolutely essential. General-purpose (GP) saddles are permitted under rules; they are simply less helpful to your position. If spending on a dressage saddle is not an option, then a GP saddle will do; it is just advisable to ride with a shorter stirrup leather to bring your legs more into alignment with the higher knee rolls.

Another option is the Working Hunter saddle which is less forward-cut than a

GP though not as straight as a dressage saddle; it is often the choice of parents for a child who will be jumping and showing their pony as well as competing in dressage.

Other Tack

Other items, such as ear covers, nose nets etc. are covered by rules and you need to check current rulings each year to see if they are permitted, or perhaps need dispensation certificates.

Condition of You and Your Horse

We touched on this earlier under 'Are you ready to compete?' in Chapter 1.

Your horse's condition will be an ongoing consideration throughout his competing life; monitoring his health, weight, fitness and soundness are all important aspects of his daily care that can impinge on his performance in competition.

Health

For a horse to be able to produce his best for you in competition, he needs not only to be healthy, but also in top form. This includes such aspects as having his teeth rasped as frequently as necessary, not just the customary once a year. Good acceptance of the bridle requires a horse to be comfortable in his mouth, and some horses need their teeth attended to as frequently as every three months. The majority will be fine with six-monthly checks, but be guided by your equine dentist or veterinary surgeon.

Feeding is another consideration: dressage requires a steady release of energy, unlike the burst of energy demanded by a racehorse. Many feed companies produce diets specifically aimed at slow, steady release of energy for horses competing in this type of discipline. If you feed straights (as opposed to compound feeds), adding good quality corn or soya oil to his feed will do the job (you will need to experiment with your individual to find which works best) with the added bonus of the sheen that this will put on his coat.

Weight

Dressage horses should be considered to be athletes and, as such, should be of an athletic build. Some horses develop heavier muscling than others and will look far more substantial, but no competition horse should carry excess fat as this puts unnecessary strain on heart, lungs and limbs. Eventers will be leaner as they are required to do more fast work whilst dressage horses do slower, more sustained power work and can be considered to be more like a weight-lifter than a sprinter, but this is still no excuse for competing an overweight, or so-called 'show-condition' animal.

Along with monitoring his weight, you will need to keep a close eye on the fit of his saddle. Horses that are being correctly trained will put on muscle bulk over the back and around the withers and shoulders, causing even the most precisely made-to-measure saddle to need frequent adjustments. The body shapes of some horses, particularly those who live out a lot, fluctuate throughout the year, and easily adjustable saddles with interchangeable head plates and adjustable air flocking have been developed to assist with these ongoing changes. However, at the end of the day it is your responsibility to notice when adjustments become necessary.

Signs that you should be aware of are: a loss of forwardness; a loss of freedom in his movement (especially in medium gaits); grumpiness about having his saddle put on; or a change in your balance making you feel like you are riding either slightly downhill or slightly uphill.

Fitness

Dressage horses *and riders* need to be fit! Completing a successful warm-up and a competition test on most horses covers anything from forty minutes to an hour of continuous riding with only short walk breaks. If you are competing in more than one test you may have little time between them. Once either of you begins to tire, your muscles will begin struggling to maintain posture and you risk both a poor performance and possible injury.

Developing and maintaining fitness can be achieved not just by masses of schooling but in a number of ways: hill work, interval training and jumping can all be used, as can (for you) swimming, cycling, aerobics, Pilates etc. Try to avoid running or jogging though, as this tends to tighten the muscles down the backs of your legs that you will want to stretch when you ride.

Other considerations for both of you to help maintain fitness are physiotherapy, chiropractic, massage and a number of other techniques such as McTimoney, Bowen and shiatsu, all of which can deal with minor muscle/joint damage at an early stage and prevent it from becoming a problem. Regular visits for both you and your horse can assist the speed of your progress by keeping injuries to a minimum. Portable massage machines for horses are also becoming more widely available, and more affordable, often in the form of a pad that you simply put on your horse and leave running on battery power. Because of their portable nature these can also be used before a warm-up, even in your horsebox at a show.

5 Competition Preparations

Careful Planning

Rules

Every competition will have rules. Make sure you have checked *which* set of rules a competition is running under, and *read them* before putting in your entry!

Remember that rules are updated annually, and some rules may be changed during the year, so you need to keep up-to-date by reading appropriate publications (e.g. *British Dressage* magazine) and/or regularly check the website of your governing body.

A Month or Two before a Show

If you compete regularly, try to plan your programme a month or two in advance. Obviously things may change that affect your plans, but you need to be aware of essential items that must be taken into consideration such as your shoeing schedule, horse vaccinations, membership and registration (or annual re-registration) for affiliated competitions, vehicle servicing and testing, not to mention your own diary! Putting such things on a wall chart or in a diary will help your planning.

Entries

Read the schedule carefully and check that both you and your horse are eligible for the classes that you want to enter. Also read the test sheets for each class and decide which are most suitable for your horse (see Chapter 3), both as a means of deciding which classes to enter and, in the event of a clash of dates, which show to go to.

Complete your entry form carefully. It will not be valid unless you have filled out all essential information such as registration numbers (if required) and signatures, and also included required items such as post-paid return envelopes and full payment!

Make sure to post your entries in plenty of time. This might sound obvious, but it is a very easy thing to put off until the last minute and not all shows take late entries. Late entries, or even a glut of entries at the closing date, can cause problems for organisers who may find themselves without sufficient judges for a show. At worst, this can result in classes being cancelled.

When you fill out your entry form also make a note in your diary of when you must ring for your times.

Staying away

For long distance venues where you intend to stay away over night or even for several days, make sure to book your stabling along with your entries: many venues are limited on stabling space and allocate on a first come first served basis, with the better stables going first.

Check the schedule carefully for information about bedding; some supply bedding with the cost of the stable, some require you to buy it; some require you to clear it totally before leaving. Different types of bedding may be offered, or you might be in temporary stables on a field, with a grass-covered floor!

If this will be your first time staying away, start to gather all the extra bits of equipment that you will need but might not already have, such as:

- An easy to pack (folding or small) wheelbarrow.

- Mucking-out tools, buckets and haynets that are spare (i.e. not required on the home yard while you are away).

- A large torch or lantern (many temporary stables have no power or lighting).

- Extra bedding (if required) for the stable.

- Conveniently packaged bales of hay or horsehage.

Even if you are used to staying away, now is the time to check that all these items are available and in good condition.

It is also advisable to **label** all items with your/your horse's name so that there can be no dispute over ownership, and you will be able to reclaim things if they get lost or left behind.

The Week before a Show

Learn your test(s)

One major stress factor for less experienced riders is the fear of forgetting the test, which adversely affects the ability to perform, and so becoming competent at memorising tests is an important skill for any competitor to develop.

There are various methods of learning dressage tests, including simply visualising the patterns, through to walking (and running!) them through on your feet. Different people learn in different ways and you will need to find out which is the most effective method for you.

- Visualising patterns – if you find the arena letters confusing, try to learn just the patterns that you will be riding without naming the markers. You may find that you can do this inside your head, or you may want to draw them on paper.

- Drawing your test – use different coloured pens for the different gaits, and perhaps an 'x' for halts. Draw a number of rectangles to represent the arena, (you can also buy ready prepared sheets of these, photocopy some of your own, or produce them on your computer) and put each movement in a new rectangle. You can either add the letters or not, depending on whether you find that helpful. Repeat the whole procedure until you can do it without referring to the test sheet. You can also purchase wipe-clean boards with both sizes of arena shown, for repetitive drawing. This technique can really help you to understand the geometry of the arena; notice the distances between the markers – they are not as helpful for your figures as you might think! (For more detail and diagrams see page 83).

- Walking the test – put out markers in the yard, or even in your living room if you have the space, and walk, trot and canter through the test on your own feet until you know it.

- Listen to it – either on CD or download it to your ipod. This way you can listen to the test repeatedly until you know it.

- Diagrammatic test plans – these are test sheets with each movement shown in diagrammatic form as well as words.

You should always ensure that you have learnt your test even if you choose to have your test commanded. This option depends on your competition: horse trials do not permit commanders, nor are they allowed at championship shows or in FEI competitions. At most regular dressage shows commanders (also known as 'readers') are allowed, but check before you rely on this assistance.

Having your test commanded can be reassuring. You have one less thing to worry about (i.e. forgetting your test), and your horse, especially if nervous, may be more relaxed with a familiar presence and voice at the side of the arena.

Noise can be a problem with commanding – strong wind or traffic/aircraft noise may make your reader hard to hear. Readers can lose their place or get behind you, or even start reading the wrong test! You may be focusing so hard on riding your horse that you fail to hear an instruction, or you may concentrate so hard on your reader's voice that you forget to ride your horse effectively. In other words, having a commander is no guarantee for not going wrong!

If you do choose to use a reader, make sure that they are either experienced or get some practice: you need them to read each movement early enough that you have sufficient time to prepare for that movement, but not get so far ahead that you get lost. They must also understand that whilst reading they should not say anything that is not on the test sheet or you may be in danger of elimination for outside assistance.

Practise your test(s)

Having chosen your test to suit the capabilities of your horse, you will need to ride through the pattern once or twice before the show. The movements in the test should all be familiar to him from your everyday schooling; if there is something a little unusual, start incorporating it into your work as soon as you have chosen the test.

Take care not to ride the full test pattern too often (definitely *not* to drill it every day) or your horse will start to anticipate and take over; transitions will no longer be under your control and movements will not necessarily be at the markers. On the other hand, riding the whole pattern at least once is necessary for you to find out where potential problems might lie.

A good three-point approach is:

1. About a week before the competition, ride through the test from start to finish, and take note of any parts that need work.

2. During the week, practise parts of the test, especially those that needed attention, but ride them in isolation, in different places in the arena and out of order so that your horse does not learn the test for himself. Remember, horses have excellent memories.

3. A day or two before the competition ride the complete test again, just to ensure that you both know it well enough not to make mistakes.

While you are practising your test, make a firm decision about which direction you will approach your entry at A: almost certainly he will be easier to get onto a straight centre line from one particular rein. Generally this will be with his stiffer side on the inside of the bend because he will not be falling outward onto his outside shoulder (much harder to straighten).

If he is fairly good at entering from either direction, then your best choice will be to come in on the same rein as you will be turning onto at the end of the centre line: e.g. if the test requires you to turn left at C, then enter from the left rein. You will already be on the correct diagonal (if you are rising to the trot), and he will anticipate a turn in the same direction even after a straight line, which will help to make the turn at C more fluent.

Another feature to take note of when practising your test is how much preparation you need to make for turns and transitions. Every horse is different, and his level of experience will also affect this estimate; a more experienced horse will react more quickly, so needing fewer steps of preparation. A truly novice horse will need plenty of time to react to your aids, and you will almost certainly find that in competition you can add at least another step or two to the time you need at home, as he will be more distracted and will take longer to notice that you are saying something to him!

On average, expect to need to start aiding a turn around three strides before the marker, an upward transition also around three steps before, and a downward transition up to five steps before the marker.

Pulling, clipping and trimming

It is well worth doing any pulling, clipping or trimming several days before the show, as a few days growth can make it look more natural. Apart from total clips, areas that might need attention are:

- Pulling his mane to an easy length for plaiting.

- Clipping his mane if he is hogged.

- Taking out a bridle patch just behind his ears (where the headpiece of the bridle lies) to separate his forelock neatly from his mane.

- Clipping a small area of mane at his withers if he has rough hair there that is impossible to incorporate into his bottom plait.

- Trimming his chin if he has a beard.

- Trimming whiskers (if you do this).

- Pulling/clipping the sides of his tail if you neither plait it nor have it full.

- Checking that his tail is not too long (length is your choice but, unless his breed demands it, an overlong tail can detract from his appearance as can an overheavy natural tail which may make him look heavy behind as opposed to athletic).

- Clipping/trimming his heels and coronets.

Telephone for times

Most shows ask you to telephone for your times two days before the competition but if it happens to be a two-day show, you might have to call three days before your class!

When you initially filled out your entry form you should have made yourself a note about calling for times because if you forget, you may find yourself eliminated. Make sure that you also note the time of day given in the schedule to call because some venues only man the telephone during particular hours. Most shows require you to call during the evening but venues such as colleges only operate during office hours. If you carry your diary with you, write down the telephone number and then you can call from wherever you are without needing to have the schedule in front of you.

Some venues allow you to check your times on a website but even some of those still require you to call to confirm that you have collected your time. Very popular venues will often hold a waiting list and any times that are not collected will be allocated to someone on that list – don't risk losing your time to anyone else by simply forgetting to call at the correct time!

If you find a conflict with your times, e.g. you have two horses in a class and not enough time between them to warm up the second horse, call or speak to the secretary *immediately*. Quite often it will be possible for them to make an adjustment, but the later you leave it the less likely this will be.

You may also be given your number. If you use a bridle or saddlecloth number, make a note of it so that you can sort out the appropriate numbers during your night-before preparation.

Check your gear

The last thing you need to find out the day before a competition is that you have a stirrup leather in need of stitching, or a glove missing.

Your tack should be checked regularly for soundness anyway, but you may have some special items that only come out for shows, such as a smart head collar or a fancy bridle. Try to make a habit of checking these items when you clean them and put them away *immediately after* a show; don't just pack them away dirty and forget about them.

If you have any new equipment, give it a trial run several days *before* a show; during the warm-up is not the time to discover that you hate your new reins, your new saddle cloth slips back under your saddle, or your horse dislikes the new bridle number beside his eye. The same applies to new clothes, but more about that in Chapter 7.

Unless you have a class that is really late in the day, it is a good idea to get all your gear together the night before. That way if you do forget something, you are much more likely to remember it overnight than when you are loading your transport just before leaving for the show.

Making a Show List can be helpful. Write down a list of everything that you might possibly want to take so that you will not be in danger of missing anything out; the list can then be pared down according to things like weather conditions when you pack. Tick items off as they are loaded, especially if more than one person is loading. Either copy or print a new list for each show or you can buy pre-prepared lists and customise them to suit your needs.

If you are stabling away, remember to include all the extras that you will need: mucking-out tools, hard feed and bulk feed (always take more than you think is sufficient), bedding (if necessary), extra rugs (temporary stabling is notoriously cold), shampoo (for those stable stains he's bound to get!), grooming and plaiting kits and a stool/step to stand on, sufficient Polos, carrots or treats to last several days, flashlight, all your own overnight gear, to include (warm) bedding and food if you are sleeping in your truck, plus something to keep you occupied during the long periods between classes.

Check your transport

Your transport needs regular checks to keep it legally roadworthy, but just before undertaking any journey when transporting a horse it is advisable to perform those checks again: oil, water, tyre conditions etc. If you have your vehicle checked by a garage or travelling mechanic make sure that you book an appointment in good time.

You should ensure that you are carrying your horse's passport and any other legal documents (e.g. an operator's licence if you have any commercial involvement) that you might need, depending upon current laws. The situation changes quite frequently, so check with the relevant authorities.

Fill up with fuel! Another potential area for stress on a competition day is the journey to the show. If road conditions are holding you up, the last thing you need is to be slowed down even further by having to pull over for fuel. If you *do* make the decision to fill up on the way, add at least five to ten minutes to your estimate for the journey time or you will undoubtedly find yourself fuming at the inexplicable queues that suddenly keep you waiting at a normally quiet fuel station.

If you have an older vehicle, it is worth checking that it will start the day before the show, particularly on cold mornings which are notoriously bad for older diesel vehicles. Turn the engine over, make sure it starts and leave it running for a while. Better yet, take it out for a run and fill up with fuel while you're out there!

Plan your journey: route and timing

If this is a venue that you visit regularly you will already know your route and how long the journey should take. If it isn't, then you need to sit down with a map and plan the journey *before* you set off, and allow extra time in case roads turn out to be slower than they look on your map. Late arrival at a show is another major stress factor and one that can easily be minimised if not totally avoided.

If you know someone who has been to this venue before, consider asking them for advice. Often a route that looks good on a map turns out not to be the most suitable one when transporting horses.

The Day before a Show

Trial and error will determine the best routine for your horse the day before a show. For some this might mean going for a hack or having a day out in the field, for others, a light work out in the school possibly running through a few movements from your test. Some horses might need to go for a gallop, others to have a full work session. Only by trialling different routines will you discover what suits him best.

There are a number of things you can do on the night before your show to save time in the morning; a great help if you have an early start!

- Try to do any bathing the day before, particularly tails and socks, but beware of washing his mane: washing, and especially conditioning, makes hair too slippery to plait easily. If you need to wash his mane, try to do this several days earlier (probably after you have pulled it). Similarly coat shine products can make the coat slippery and so beware of putting them where your saddle and girth sit!

- Rug him (appropriate to weather conditions) as far as possible to help keep him clean overnight, especially if he is turned out.

- Separate his mane ready for plaiting, and leave in bunches held in rubber bands.

- Alternatively, if you want to plait the night before (and you know he won't rub them out), just leave the bottom two or three plaits by his withers undone: if you don't, when he puts his head down these bottom plaits will pull loose or may even rip out the hair at the roots.

- Clean your tack, riding boots and (if you wear them) spurs, and if possible load everything onto your transport. Even if you don't want to load valuable items because of security concerns, load everything else and put those last minute items together ready for the morning.

- If you have been given a number (if the show is affiliated you will have collected your number along with your time) and you use either a bridle or saddle cloth number, change the number from the one you had at your last show to the new one, and attach it to the appropriate place.

- Fill hay nets ready for travelling in both directions, and an extra one to take with you if you are going to be out all day.

- Check that you have water loaded – either in your lorry's water supply or in a container – together with buckets for drinking and washing down.

- Plan your timetable for the morning and set your alarm!

Again, be guided by the experience you gain over a number of shows as to how much you can do with your horse by way of preparation the night before. For example, if he becomes agitated by associating plaiting with something he finds exciting or stressful, i.e. a show, you will just have to leave it until the morning, as you might have to also leave washing his socks and/or tail. Take note of his behaviour and tailor your preparations to keep him as relaxed as possible.

On the Morning of a Show

Always allow sufficient extra time for things to go wrong: dirty socks that need washing again, plaits that won't sit how you want them to, the horse who has found the only patch of mud in an otherwise dry field!

If you are used to having help and you suddenly find yourself going to a show alone, be aware that it takes *more than twice the time to do things alone*; doing twice the work means that you will do it more slowly!

If at all possible, try to leave children and dogs at home. You will have enough to think about without the extra responsibilities of other bodies while you are trying to get ready to ride.

Make a final check before you leave to ensure that you have loaded all vital items: your tack, your riding clothes and hat and your horse – believe me, people have been known to forget the horse!

Plan to arrive at the show *at least* one hour before your time (this is assuming that your warm-up takes half an hour). If you are fairly new to competing, or your horse takes a while to settle in strange surroundings, or the venue is new to you, plan on a little longer; the worst thing you can do is to be short of time; once you start to rush things your horse will sense a problem and you will have sabotaged your performance before you are even mounted.

6 Arrival at the Show

Having an exact routine and sticking to it can be a great help with any competition nerves and will help ensure that you don't forget anything. It may take you a few shows to develop this routine, but below is a basic framework for you to start from.

Once you are parked and your horse is settled (if you use a portable battery powered massage pad as part of his warm-up routine, now might be the best time to put it on and set it to work) your first item on the agenda will be to check the layout of the showground. You will want to locate the following:

- Secretary

- Scoreboards

- Warm-up arena

- Competition arena(s)

- Toilets

- Refreshments

Show Routine

Declarations

Always start with a visit to the secretary to find out if you need to declare your intention to compete: this may be by putting a tick beside your name on the scoreboard, or by speaking to the secretary. Verify your riding times at this point – sometimes mistakes can occur when times are given out over the telephone – and check the location and order of the arena(s) in which you will be competing.

If you know that certain judges or competitors will make you anxious, ask someone else to look at the board for you.

This is also an opportunity to collect your number (either from the secretary or from the scoreboard) if you have not previously done so, and to ask such questions as:

- Are you allowed to ride without a jacket in hot weather?

- Are you allowed to go *inside* the arena before the bell rings? This is not always a clear-cut issue at certain venues, so get a definitive answer while you can.

- Is your class, or the class before yours, running to time? You do not want to find halfway through your warm-up that the show is running half an hour late. If a show has ring stewards you will also be able to check this whilst in the warm-up arena, but many shows are self-stewarding and, owing to many and varied reasons, classes may well not run to time despite the precise riding time that you have been allocated. On the other hand, bear in mind that classes can unpredictably catch up time by judges missing out on breaks both within and between classes, and owing to withdrawals.

- If you are unsure, check whether you are allowed a whip in your class. Certain classes (such as championships) have a no-whip rule, not always made clear on the printed schedule.

- If you are competing in a music class, now is the time to hand in your CD.

Show Etiquette

Be sensible and courteous whilst on the showground and take note of any particular rules specific to the venue such as:

- No dogs outside your vehicle.

- Pick up your horse's droppings.

- Do not leave your horse unattended whilst he is tied to your vehicle.

- Pick up and take away your rubbish – this includes such items as plaiting bands when you have finished competing: you may be parked on someone's grazing field.

If, for any reason, you need to scratch from a class, do so as soon as you can – the show may be able to fit another competitor into the vacant slot, and one day you may benefit from this yourself.

Pre-warm up Strategies

You may find it helpful to allow time to watch a few competitors ride the test before you finish getting ready. You can only do this if there is enough time to fit it in but, if not, at least take yourself to the arena and stand as near as you can, then *visualise* the test, riding through every movement in your mind.

Now is *not* the time for socialising: save that for after your ride.

Planning your warm-up

Once you know the layout of the showground you can plan more precisely the time you should be mounting. At some venues the warm-up arena may be some way from the lorry park, and/or the competition arena can be several minutes walk away from the warm-up arena. Either of these routes may include an obstacle course of anything from mobile tack shops with generators running to getting past ponds full of ducks and geese! Add any extra time that you might need for these obstacles to your planned warm-up time in order to arrive at a scheduled mounting time.

Trial and error will also be involved in determining how long you need for getting ready before mounting. This will also be affected by extra issues such as the weather (more clothes to change when it's cold) and by how many assistants you have with you, and how experienced they are, or if you are solo. You can certainly reduce this time by wearing most of your riding clothes for the journey (try to cover up with overclothes to stay clean), but you will still need time for tacking up which, as this is a prime moment for conveying anxiety to your horse, should always be done calmly and without rushing.

Make sure that you have everything with you

If you are on your own, you will have to make your final preparations before you mount, wear all your gear and put anything else that you might need into your pockets! If, as is more likely, you have an assistant with you, she can carry all those last minute things that you may need after you have mounted:

- Riding jacket.

- Bottle of water.

- Test sheet – for reader or for last minute checks.

- Polos/treats.

- Whip and/or spurs if you can't decide before mounting what you might need in the motivational department.

- Sun cream (for either or both you and your horse).

- Fly repellent.

- Sponges, grooming kits etc. for last minute smartening up.

- Raincoat.

So, having organised yourself and your horse and arrived at the warm-up arena at your planned time, you are now ready to start.

Warm-up Strategies

Why warm up?

A thorough warm-up before doing any demanding work is **absolutely essential** both for the best performance possible and to avoid joint and/or muscle injuries. You will never see athletes, gymnasts or dancers perform without a comprehensive warm-up routine, so why should you expect your horse, who has to be all three of these performers rolled into one, to do otherwise.

Trying to start your ride in the outline that you want for competition can not only potentially cause physical damage but, because of the discomfort induced, may also result in your horse losing confidence in you. This might be manifest in a variety of behaviour patterns ranging from not going forward to spooking or running away. If difficult behaviour is an issue for you at shows, consider your warm-up routine as a possible cause.

The term 'warm up' literally describes the physical warming of his muscles and joints. Increased exercise produces heat within his muscles as a result of aerobic respiration – the breakdown of certain chemicals within his muscles as a result of interacting with oxygen – which produces energy (muscle activity) and heat. His body will respond to the increased demand for oxygen with a faster breathing rate, increased blood flow (the heart pumps faster) and vasodilation (the enlargement of the blood vessels). This results in more available oxygen for energy production, expanded muscles and better lubricated joints, giving him a more toned posture and greater elasticity of movement.

The duration and content of a warm-up will vary depending upon many factors, including temperature and weather conditions, the temperament of your horse, and surface and space in the warm-up arena. If you are competing with a view to winning a class, getting the warm-up just right is often what makes the difference between winning and placing, and so perfecting your warm-up is a must!

To give us a good foundation, let's consider what could be termed an 'ideal' warm-up, in ideal conditions.

The ideal warm-up

To bring an average horse to peak performance readiness without tiring him should take around thirty to thirty-five minutes broken down into the following three sections.

1. Loosening/stretching work.

2. Putting your horse on the aids.

3. Working through movements.

Loosening/stretching work   This should begin with eight minutes of walking – the time shown by scientific studies to bring a horse's muscles up to working temperature. The first four or five minutes should be on a long rein with him reaching downward/forward towards the bit in a long but round outline, allowing him to become totally relaxed and familiar with his surroundings. Much of this will be going large around the perimeter of the arena, although not on the track if other riders are working at a faster pace than you, but also include a few large circles to stretch him laterally as well as longitudinally.

For the remainder of the walk period start to take a little contact, but still in a long and stretched frame. If appropriate to his level of training, you can incorporate some leg-yielding to start tuning him in to your leg aids. Before you move on to trot take a moment to check your girth. Once you move into the trot, still in a stretched frame with a longish rein, start to ride a variety of patterns involving frequent changes of direction, which challenge his balance and attention so keeping him interested and waking up his postural muscles. Have a brief canter on each rein, still in a long frame, and then come back to walk to give him a short breather and to re-check your girth. This whole section should have taken around fifteen minutes.

Starting the warm-up: a relaxed walk in a long but rounded outline: the author with Lover Boy (Stanley). As this was a winter's day Stanley is wearing a quarter sheet (see Cold Weather on page 64) of a design that can be easily removed without the need to dismount.

Putting your horse on the aids This next phase involves gaining your horse's undivided attention to enable you to fully engage him both mentally and physically and so once you are ready to recommence work, take up your reins a little shorter than before, but not yet as short as you will ultimately want them. Put him up to either trot or canter, depending on which is his better gait, and start to ride transitions, both between the gaits and within the gaits. As his outline shortens (which will happen during downward transitions if they are ridden correctly), gradually take the reins shorter until you have them at your normal working length. With some horses, smaller circles and lateral work are an alternative way to work him from your legs into your contact, or use a mix of all these techniques. This section should take around five minutes, but must be as long as it needs to be; moving on to practising movements before he is ready will cause tension and stress, destroying confidence in both of you.

Working through movements   For the final ten minutes or so of your warm-up, run through one or two of your test movements. You should know from your trial runs at home which movements he might need to be reminded about: possibly medium strides, smaller circles, any lateral work and almost certainly a centre line or two, with or without a halt depending on whether he is inclined to anticipate (don't practise the halt) or run through the bridle (do practise the halt). *You do not need to practise everything in the test.*

Allow time for the last-minute checks – ensure that the girth is tight and the straps tucked in, put on your jacket, take off bandages/boots – and to get to the arena which may be several minutes walk away. Depending on his temperament, he may benefit from a short rest, in which case you will need to add the time to your thirty minutes, or he may work best if, after your final preparations, you do a couple more transitions and then trot (if allowed) to the arena without letting him come off your aids.

> **Note**
> It takes two minutes for a horse's muscles to recover from strenuous work – this is the time shown in scientific studies for the muscles to be re-oxygenated ready to resume work – so use this as a guideline for your rest periods. Hint: one and a half times around the perimeter of a 20 x 60 m arena in walk on an average horse takes approximately two minutes; try timing how long it takes yours.

Whilst the above outline is ideal, it may not be suitable for your horse. Very excitable horses and very lazy ones may need totally different approaches, and prevailing conditions may also require you to use alternative strategies and adjust both the patterns and time schedule from this ideal.

Alternative strategies: weather variations
Cold weather

If at all possible, use a quarter sheet in really cold weather to help keep his back muscles warm (see photograph on page 62).

Use a sheet that is designed to be removed without you having to dismount, as you will probably discard it about halfway through your warm-up, when he is ready to do some hard work.

In really cold weather you may need to shorten or even cut out the walk period at the start of your warm-up. Clearly this is not ideal, as you will be making demands on cold, tight muscles, but in really low temperatures he may be getting colder rather than warmer when you walk, or he may be feeling silly because of the chill, making walk a rather unsafe option!

Rising trot and/or cantering in light seat may have to replace the walk section, if it is safe enough to do so, using as long a rein and outline as sensible under the circumstances. You may even need a fairly short rein if he is feeling sharp, moving on to stretching him once he starts to warm up and relax.

Under these conditions, keep walk periods to a minimum and consider having his quarter sheet placed over his haunches during each walk period, although this is only really feasible when you have assistance. If you are on your own, you will probably want to keep the sheet on until he is thoroughly warmed up and ready to get into the last section of your programme.

Hot weather

Your warm-up in hot weather can potentially be shortened as his muscles will already be warmer at the start, and most horses are more relaxed when they are hot.

Shortening the loosening-up phase and doing a bare minimum of competition movements will allow you to retain more energy for your test; overdoing the warm-up in hot weather can easily cause excess sweating, leading to a degree of dehydration that may be sufficient to reduce his energy and performance.

Consider giving him a longer break between finishing your warm-up and going to the competition arena to help him recover his energy levels. With some horses this may even be a half hour rest back in the horsebox or anywhere in the shade. If he has been well educated you should be able to pick him up in just a few minutes (see page 41) with a small number of transitions and be ready to go within five minutes of remounting.

Obviously if your intention is to give him a rest period after your warm-up you will need to allow for this in your planned arrival time at the show.

Heavy rain

You may want to treat a warm-up in very wet conditions the same as for the cold-weather warm-up described above. Very heavy rain can be chilling, and a waterproof sheet may help. On the other hand if it is warm and wet beware of getting either of you too hot by putting on extra gear; you are going to get wet anyway, so don't add to your discomfort!

Alternative strategies: differing temperaments
The excitable horse

With this type of horse it is even more important that you really know what suits him best. You are facing probably three possibilities:

1. Do the ideal warm-up and try to keep him feeling calm and unpressurised.

2. Ride a really long warm-up until he is tired enough to be sensible and cooperative.

3. Do a really short warm-up which gives him no time to become stressed.

The ideal warm-up This might have to be *tailored to suit* an eager, very forward horse and will involve the smart use of patterns, keeping him always on the turn and focussing inward toward the centre of the school so that he has no real opportunity to look around and become excited. The walk phase will depend on how calm your individual horse is about walk: some horses are relaxed about the walk, only becoming excitable as they go into faster gaits (in which case, do the walk as described for the ideal warm-up), whilst some are impossible to keep calm in walk and you may need to go straight into trot or canter, whichever keeps him calmer, as described above in the cold-weather warm-up. In the second phase of your warm-up, be governed in your choice of exercises by whatever keeps him most calm: either transitions or lateral work, and if he finds particular movements from the test exciting, then it is probably best to avoid them in the warm-up altogether.

The long warm-up In some cases a long warm-up may be suitable, but is not a good choice if you can find another way. Unless he is supremely fit you will actually be gaining cooperation only by making him tired, which means that he will not be in an ideal situation either physically or mentally to produce his best work.

The short warm-up In the case of those horses who become more excited the longer you ride them, a really short warm-up of around 15 minutes – just long enough to warm and supple the muscles – may be most suitable. If your horse is one of those who becomes more and more excitable with each subsequent canter, you can even consider not cantering at all in the warm-up; just walk and trot a little and leave his first, and best, canter for the test. If you are a little dubious about his first canter transition, then just make one transition in the warm-up and canter no more than a half 20 m circle, leaving the next one for the competition arena.

I have even worked with one excitable event horse who produced his best work with no warm-up at all: he was led to the competition arena and only mounted when it was his turn to go in! Clearly this is not desirable, but is a good example of how treating every horse as an individual, and experimenting with the warm-up, can help you to discover how to produce the best possible performance from every horse.

The lazy horse

You will have two goals with this type of horse:

1. To get him as responsive, on your aids, as you can.

2. To conserve energy.

Try adapting the ideal warm-up by shortening the last phase so that you avoid wearing him out, and making more transitions during the second phase. Use plenty of transitions *within* the gaits and plenty of trot to canter transitions, as these will help him to be more forward thinking. When you ask for a transition, demand a sharp response and if he fails to give you what you want, keep using a stronger aid until you get it.

With some lazy horses it can be better to go for a hack to warm up, rather than going into an arena. Obviously this depends on the venue, but it is certainly a viable option if feasible.

Before you label your horse as 'lazy', be sure that this is genuinely the case: a nervous horse can lack forwardness as a result of mental and physical tension. This horse will hold his muscles too tightly, which will not enable him to go forward. He must be encouraged to relax by you sitting quietly and not over-riding him, which would only make him rush and become tenser. Once he has relaxed and 'let go' he will move forward willingly on his own.

The inattentive horse

Inattention may be due to anxiety from working in close proximity to other horses, a strange environment, insecurity about his balance, lack of submission to you etc. You should try to understand what is causing this as it is something you need to rectify before you bring him out in public again.

The way you warm him up will be pretty much the same regardless of why he is inattentive, but you may need to modify some of your demands depending on that reason. If he is genuinely anxious you must take care not to make him feel pressurised, or he may react in an unpredictable manner; you are trying to gain his confidence, not to frighten him. If, on the other hand, he is just not sufficiently on your aids to listen to you, you can – and must – be a lot more demanding.

Take a slightly shorter rein from the start on this horse, though still long enough to allow him to stretch a little. You may need to move to the second phase of brisk and varied transitions much earlier so that he cannot predict what you are going to ask and as a consequence will find it necessary to listen to you. Make frequent small circles, changes of direction and also (especially with the nervous horse) spirals, all of which focus him towards the inside of the arena giving him less opportunity to look out and be distracted.

Trying to establish a genuine connection between your legs and the bridle is your goal with this horse, so that even if he wants to look around he is sufficiently on your aids that you can tell him, 'focus on *me*'. This will be of utmost import when you move to the competition arena and he has a whole new environment to cope with. If you are able, try using shoulder-in or shoulder-fore around the outside of the arena before entering and, indeed, inside it (see tactics for coping with spooking in the arena on page 97), to keep him connected and, as a consequence, attentive to *you*, not to his surroundings.

The Iberian warm-up

An example of other possibilities includes a variant on the warm-up that is that favoured by many trainers of Iberian horses. This involves basically the same phases and patterns as described for the ideal warm-up, but with everything done in shoulder-in positioning, performed equally in both directions, of course. This includes even the long-rein work done at the start, the goal being to fully engage first one hind leg, then the other, by placing them in turn fully beneath his body. I have used this to good effect with one particularly idle Warmblood mare, finding her far more forward for far less effort using this particular technique.

Other considerations

Apart from weather conditions and individual temperaments, other factors that you may need to take into account could be:

- The age of your horse: older horses will require longer limbering up at the start, but may need less specific test preparation as they are, probably, more experienced. Young horses may run out of energy quite quickly, and your warm-up estimate may be closer to 20 minutes rather than 30 minutes.

- How your horse lives: a fully stabled horse will need longer to loosen up than one who lives in a field or has long periods of turn-out, especially if he has slept out the night before your show.

- His build: a more heavily muscled horse will need longer in the first stage of the warm-up to bring his muscles up to working temperature, simply because he has more muscle bulk to warm up!

- The length of your journey to the show: a long journey may make him stiffer than a short one, and so a longer time spent on the first phase may be beneficial. One the other hand, a long journey might also make him more tired, so you may want to plan a shorter warm-up.

Listen to your horse

Even knowing your horse well, and knowing which form of warm-up suits him the best, it is still important to ascertain at the start of a warm-up *how he feels today*.

There are so many factors that can influence a horse's mood, and you cannot control them all, so it is your job when you start to ride *not* to let your mind go into neutral ('Just another warm-up, yawn') or allow yourself to be distracted by the surroundings or by having a chat with your friends, but to take note of how your horse *feels*: sharper than usual, lazier than usual, distracted, on the ball?

When you know how he feels you can adapt your demands/responses to suit his mood of the day and have the best possible chance of a truly harmonious ride.

Tune in your mental focus

To achieve this awareness means that for *you*, one of the most important aspects of the warm-up is to tune in your mental focus. The most successful riders appear to be oblivious to their surroundings – and to a large extent, they really are! They are focussing solely on the feelings that they are getting from their horse and not on their surroundings, other competitors, or even the weather. Try to catch their eye and you'll find that you can't: they are only aware of you enough not to run into you!

Achieving this form of concentration takes practice, but is certainly possible for anyone to learn. Key steps in the process are learning to:

- Leave any mental 'baggage' behind when you mount – take a deep breath and put all those things that are on your mind (bills you have to pay, a time you have to be home, the meal you are planning etc.) on hold. Anything that distracts you from absolute attention to your horse when you are riding has no place inside the arena. With practice you will find that you can leave all unnecessary clutter out of your mind until your boots are back on solid ground.

- Defocus your eyes so that you are not looking directly at either your horse's neck or at other competitors. (See below for more on this technique.)

- Switch on your most effective mental 'state'. (See Chapter 2.)

- Know your dominant sense: visual (seeing), auditory (hearing) or kinesthetic (feeling), and develop templates that suit *you*. For example, describing awareness of rhythm in her book *Score More For Dressage* (J. A. Allen, 2006), Wendy Jago says: 'Feel it like a heartbeat, if you are kinesthetic. Hear it like a metronome, if you are auditory. Or, if you are visual, imagine yourself tracing the line of your rise and fall in the air in front of your surroundings like the regular peaks and troughs on a monitor screen.'

- Concentrate on making things as easy as possible for your horse; plan ahead for everything from turning corners to changing gaits.

Defocussing your visual input

As you are riding, imagine a tennis ball floating in the air at eye level and about 3 m in front of you. Focus your eyes on the imaginary ball and continue to do so as your ride. The ball will always stay at the same height and distance in front of you, so your focus will not change.

Notice when you do this that you still have clear, though slightly fuzzy, peripheral vision, enough that you won't run into anyone else in the warm-up arena, yet not sharp enough for you to really *see* your fellow competitors and be either distracted or intimidated by what they are doing.

Many riders try, either consciously or unconsciously, to achieve this level of concentration by focussing down onto their horse's neck and so blocking out peripheral vision entirely. Whilst this will allow you to see the position of his head and neck, you cannot use it as a true measure of whether he is on the bit or not, as this is not solely dependent upon head position, and it will both overload his forehand, because your head inclines slightly forward, and make you prone to crashes with other competitors as you fail to see where you, or they, are going!

Rules of the warm-up arena

Bear in mind that in the warm-up you can only use the same saddle and bridle that you are permitted to use in competition. Neck straps may be allowed in the warm-up, but check the appropriate rule book. Boots and bandages are allowed but must be removed before entering the competition arena. You are permitted to carry one whip (but not two)in the warm-up even if it must be dropped before going into the competition arena.

- When you enter the warm-up arena, be careful not to cut off another rider. In the case of entering an indoor arena it may be a good idea to warn other riders by calling out: 'Coming in', or something similar.

- When riding at a slower gait, especially at walk, or if you intend to halt, take the inner track and allow riders working at trot or canter to pass you on the outside track.

- Once you are working at trot or canter, pass other riders left hand to left hand *unless* the other rider is in counter-canter, in which case you should circle away.

- Look where you are going!

- Always keep one horse's length away from other horses – in all directions!

- When overtaking riders going in the same direction, pass on the inside with plenty of clearance. Better yet, circle away or cut across the arena to avoid overtaking.

- When turning or halting, always check behind you first.

- Take care how you use your whip – other horses may react more enthusiastically than your own! Also, take care that it doesn't hit the face of a horse coming in the opposite direction. Try not to carry an excessively long whip as this makes it more difficult to avoid accidentally hitting other horses.

- Always be courteous and polite, everyone has the same right to be there.

- Take extra care around more novice horses and riders – give them more space. The same applies to horses wearing ribbons in their tails: red indicates they might kick; green states they are novice horses. Riders of stallions may wear a yellow cross band and it is also advisable to give these riders more space, especially if you are on a mare!

- Stop and stand still, or stay in one area, when another rider has serious trouble or loses control.

- Perform your warm-up routine with a purpose: do not meander around the arena.

- When adjusting any equipment, e.g. tightening your girth, stand in the middle of the arena or, if you need assistance, leave the arena; do not ask your assistant to step in, having people on their feet in a warm-up arena is dangerous and disruptive to those still trying to work around you. The same applies to your last moment preparations: putting jackets on and taking off boots etc.

- Do not school after a test if you are angry.

- Many shows where you are stabled away from home require your horse to wear a bridle number whenever he is out of the stable, regardless of whether you are actually preparing for a class or just schooling him on a non-competing day. Be aware of such rules.

- Do not attempt to lunge in the warm-up arena.

- If you are working in the arena but not due to compete (your class may be later in the day, or on the following day) you must give way to riders who are due into the arena.

Arriving at the arena on time
Stewards

If your show uses ring stewards you should make yourself known to them around 15 minutes before your competing time. They may already have identified you when you entered the warm-up arena but it is up to you to ensure that they know who you are.

At some shows, especially championship shows, there may be a steward responsible for tack checks and you must take a moment out of your warm-up to allow them to perform this: they will specifically be looking at your spurs and your horse's bit(s) and noseband to ensure that they comply with the rules for your class. Alternatively these checks may be performed after you have completed your test.

A ring steward should keep you informed during the last few minutes of your warm-up about how soon you will be required to go into the competition arena, but if they don't volunteer information, then ask them: ultimately it is your responsibility to be on time.

Self-stewarding/last few minutes

During the last section of your warm-up try to keep a check on how the class is running. If there is no steward – many shows are self-stewarding – keep an eye on the numbers of the two or three horses before you in the running order. Many warm-up arenas have a running order posted nearby, or you could send a helper to check numbers. Identify those competitors as you ride, and as each of them leaves the warm-up arena you can get a more precise estimate of exactly when your turn will be. As mentioned earlier, classes often do not run to time and, even when there is a steward present, this is your best way of estimating how much warm-up time you have left. Even when a class appears to be running late, it may catch up very quickly as a result of withdrawals, or judges curtailing their breaks, so by being continually aware of those competitors ahead of you, you will not be caught out.

Final checks

Before making your way from the warm-up arena to the competition arena ensure that you are totally ready. Any or all of the following may be necessary:

- Put on your jacket and gloves.

- If you use them, remove boots/bandages.

- If you have used radio equipment for working with your trainer, make sure you remove it now.

- Final girth check and tuck straps in.

- Final sponge/wipe over to make him look as good as possible.

- Wipe any dust off your boots.

- Apply a new layer of fly repellent.

- A sweet – Polo or sugar – may be appropriate if he expects one!

- Make a last-minute mental run through of your test pattern.

- Get into your positive mindset using either of the techniques suggested on page 22, and remember the important goal of giving your *horse* the best possible experience inside the arena that you can.

- Make your way to the arena, confident in the knowledge that you are as well prepared as possible.

Boots and bandages

Especially if you are on your own, consider carefully whether you *really* need to use boots or bandages for your warm-up, or are they just a fashion statement?

Forgetting to remove boots or bandages is probably the number one reason for elimination in dressage competitions (the other major one is forgetting to drop your whip when going into a class where whips are not permitted), and even grooms forget about them sometimes!

Unless he is liable to knock himself, or maybe throw himself around in a temper tantrum in the warm-up arena, you might be better not putting them on in the first place. This is even more relevant when at a competition on your own, where you would have to either ask a spectator to do it for you or dismount to remove them yourself.

Riding ahead of your allotted time

Sometimes a class may run early, or the competitor before you has scratched. When you find yourself in this situation, *do not* feel pressurised, or let a steward pressurise you, into going in ahead of your time *unless you are ready to do so*. You are *under no obligation to ride before your time*, but once you present yourself at the arena you are declaring that you are ready to be judged, so unless you are indeed ready, stick to your allotted time and make full use of your warm-up time.

If you *do* opt to ride early, when you feel further warm-up time is unhelpful, you may do so. The judge will be aware that you are riding ahead of time, but what they *will not do* is give you extra time to ride around the arena before ringing the bell, so do not expect to continue your warm-up once you arrive at the competition arena.

If you are scheduled to ride immediately after a judging break, *do not* go to the arena early. You must not arrive before the judge returns; it is unfair to other competitors to take extra time to familiarise your horse with the competition arena and you risk elimination by doing so.

7 Presentation

Appearance

In dressage, presentation is the name of the game: you need to give the judge the confidence that you know what you are doing, even if you're not so sure yourself!

The judge's first sight of you will be as you arrive in the competition arena to ride around before starting your test. The more confident and professional an appearance you present, the more confidence the judge will have in your ability to present your horse in a capable manner.

Riding Wear

Clothing is an image-maker, especially in dressage; it is a reflection of your attention to detail and it affects the way that you ride.

Before going to a show, try having a dress rehearsal at home; not only will you be sure that you are comfortable in all your show gear (is your underwear up to the job?), you will also find out if anything needs changing, e.g. gloves that slip on the reins, or mending, e.g. jacket buttons coming loose, or something new that needs more wearing in.

Notice how much better you ride in your show gear; your posture and self-awareness are improved and, as a result, your horse's attention to you is better. If you *know* you look good, you will feel more of that positive mental attitude we talked about in Chapter 2.

Fashions come and go, but a neat appearance is a must. Loose pony tails (on ladies or gentlemen!), dangling earrings or dirty boots are all unnecessary and serve only to give an impression of sloppiness. There will always be the odd exception in the cleanliness stakes, in terrible weather or knee deep mud in the horsebox park, but under most circumstances such a lack of attention to detail suggests that lack might also pervade other areas, such as your horse's training.

The current rule book for your sport will determine exactly what you wear in terms of hat, jacket, spurs etc. Rules differ between dressage, horse trials, pony clubs and riding clubs, and are updated every year so you will need to check at the start of each season to see what you are permitted. Within those limitations, and the depth of your pocket, you should choose as well-tailored clothing as you can find. Clothing that is too tight (too many Christmas lunches) or too loose (because you also wear that jacket to show jump with a body protector underneath) detracts from the aesthetics of your appearance, and whilst you may feel that this should not be an issue as the judge 'should be looking at the horse', it *does* affect the overall image that you present.

Stocks

If you wear a stock, tie it neatly and secure the loose ends with safety pins so that they cannot come out of your jacket and flap around. The pins will not be visible beneath your jacket.

Use discreetly placed safety pins to hold the ends of your stock in place.

Jackets

Jackets should always be worn except on those occasions when you may be permitted to ride without a jacket because the weather is very hot. Always check with the organiser upon arrival to confirm that this is permitted, no matter how hot *you* think it is.

If you are riding without a jacket, your shirt should be plain white *and must have sleeves*, either long or short. If you are still wearing a stock, it is even more important that it is fastened down. Try to put the safety pins in from under your shirt so that you just have a short bar showing as opposed to the entire pin (see photograph above).

Gloves

Requirements in terms of colour may change through the years but if you are free to choose, consider carefully: white or pale-coloured gloves draw the eye. If you have lovely quiet, still hands then by all means wear pale-coloured gloves, they look good and can add to your image of competence as you show what an excellent contact you have.

If, on the other hand (so to speak!), you have problems keeping your hands still, white or pale gloves are not for you. Black, brown or any dark colour that will not draw the judge's eye should be your choice. You can always colour-coordinate them with your jacket or your horse.

Hats

You have a choice of hat styles, so choose the one that you are most comfortable with.

Some rules require a safety hat with harness and as this is certainly acceptable under all rules choose a shape that suits you, a colour to match your jacket and an unobtrusive harness. If you wear a crash cap with a cover, ensure that the cover is as well fitted to the cap as possible, not just perched on top, and is still a strong colour – they fade easily.

Hair nets

Unless your hair is *really* short you should wear a hair net for neatness. Even a very lightweight net will stop stray short bits of hair from sticking out, particularly when a top hat or bowler is worn, when more of your hair is exposed than with an ordinary riding hat.

If your hair is long, consider putting a band around the net to make a short, contained ponytail.

 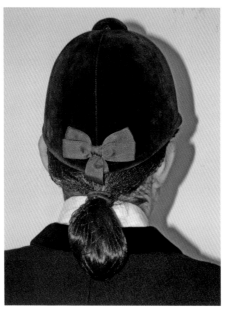

(*Left*) Long hair in a net but without a band can easily become lopsided and look messy. (*Right*) A hair net worn with a ponytail band is neat and tidy.

Your goal is to contain your hair enough that it doesn't bounce against your back. Bouncing hair of any description is very distracting and can really draw the judge's eye away from what you are trying to present: your horse.

Riding boots

Whilst this is an item most often dictated by your finances, do bear in mind that a taller boot improves the look of any shape of leg, making it appear longer and more elegant. Boots that come only just to the top of your calves, or showing boots with garter straps are perfectly acceptable but will never create the same aesthetic look as a tall boot that curves upward, with a Spanish-cut top, at the side of your knee.

If you have difficulty getting tall boots to fit, many makes now come with zips for ease of putting on and taking off, and under some rules you are permitted short boots with matching gaiters which should also be chosen for their tall, elegant silhouette.

Accessories

Whips

Whips are not permitted in all classes; again it is important that you check the appropriate rule book before assuming that you can carry one.

A long schooling whip is most appropriate although some rule books dictate a maximum length and so, again, check first. A short whip that requires you to remove your hand from the reins to use it is only really appropriate on a youngster who has not yet been introduced to the longer version. In a test you want to show as little as you can in the way of visible aids.

If riding indoors, or in an arena with close-boarded sides, you may want to consider riding *without* a whip altogether. Scraping the whip against the wall can be distracting and the noise may even spook your horse. If you choose to carry one in such an arena you will really need to keep turning it over so that you have it always on the inside, away from the wall. (See the series of photographs on page 95 showing how to turn the whip over correctly.)

Spurs

Spurs may be permitted, not permitted, or compulsory, depending on the class that you are competing in, and certain styles are not permitted, so check that rule book!

Spurs should be fitted so that they lie along, or only just beneath, the seam of your boot where the foot of the boot joins the leg. Drooping spurs or spurs fitted lower than this will not be easy to bring into contact with your horse's sides, and mean that you will tend to bring your heels up to use them, destroying your leg, and consequently your seat, position.

Ordinary spurs correctly fitted, lying parallel to, and not far below, the seam of the boot.

Swan-necked spurs which curve upward, allowing a long-legged rider contact with a shallow-barrelled horse. These are not ordinary spurs worn upside-down, which is not permitted.

If you wear spurs, try not to use them at every stride, they should be there as an aid for that little bit of extra response, not just to keep your horse going. Poking him with spurs at every stride not only makes it obvious to the judge that he lacks impulsion but will also serve to further deaden him to your legs.

Horse Turnout

It should go without saying that your horse should be as clean and tidy as you can make him. He should be fully groomed, with white legs/patches washed, and trimmed as befits his type.

As with your choice of clothing and tack, his exact turnout is a matter for your individual choice.

- Manes: to plait or not to plait? There is no absolute requirement to plait (braid) a mane, but it will certainly give a better impression if you do so, unless his breed dictates otherwise. The style of plaiting is up to you: number, shape, position and/or white tape, can all be used with horses of different conformations to enhance the arch of the neck.

- Tails: full, pulled, plaited or with the sides shaved, is up to you, but no matter how it is presented a tail should always be clean and combed/brushed out.

- Heels: look best trimmed unless his breed requires feathers, as the neater silhouette makes for a more elegant image.

- Other body hair: trimming chins, whiskers etc. is, again, up to you, just bear in mind that a really hairy chin will make his head look heavy.

First Impressions

Before the bell

Having fully organised you, your horse and both of your wardrobes, and knowing that you look as good as you possibly can, now you can make a positive first impression upon the judge by riding confidently around the arena prior to the signal for you to start (which might be a bell, horn, buzzer, whistle or even just the judge's voice).

Start by going straight to the judge's car/box to show your number to the judge/writer, and then use what time you have left as productively as possible.

So, what can you do with these last few seconds before you must begin your test? You have a choice and it should be based upon your horse's temperament. You might:

- Trot quietly around the ring, allowing him to familiarise himself with his surroundings.

- Canter around if he is a bit anxious, allowing him to release some nervous energy in the extra forwardness of the faster gait.

- Take him back and forth past a particularly spooky object to desensitise him to it.

- Make lots of transitions to keep him alert and listening to you.

- Practise a few halts.

- Walk around to conserve energy.

Just because the majority of people trot aimlessly around the ring, don't feel that you must do so too! Make the most of these last moments; once you are in that ring you have no more practice time.

If you are allowed to enter the arena before the bell, **do so**! Take every opportunity that you are offered to familiarise him with the ring. Finding out that he takes exception to one corner, or to the judge's car *after* you have started, and you failed to take the opportunity offered to you to ride him in there before the test, is foolhardy.

When you arrived you should have checked whether or not you are allowed to ride-in inside the ring; the construction of some arenas means that you may have to enter some or all of it prior to the bell. On the other hand, entering *before* the bell when this is not permitted will result in elimination, so be sure: ask beforehand!

After the bell

Once the judge has signalled for you to start, you must enter the arena within the permitted time (check your rule book). There will be no further signal to warn you that you are running out of time, so without either panicking or hurrying your horse, try to enter the arena by the most direct route possible after the bell.

Do not attempt to ride another full circuit of the arena even if you feel that this might help your horse to be more relaxed: it won't help if you have been eliminated!

If, for any reason, you are not sure whether you heard the bell, or are uncertain it was the bell for your arena (this is often confusing where multiple arenas are adjacent to each other), *look at the judge*: they will confirm if they have done so, usually verbally or by nodding their head.

Presenting the Test as a Whole

First impressions are important, but so also will be your ability to deal quickly and effectively with any problems that occur during a test, without letting them affect the remainder of the test.

Even if you have never show-jumped, you have probably heard television commentators bemoaning the inexperience of the rider who looks back at a jump they have just knocked down, as this takes their concentration, and the all-important directional focus of their eyes, off the remainder of the course, and almost always precedes further errors. Riding a dressage test should be viewed in the same way: if you make a mistake by either going wrong or riding a movement badly, *do not* dwell on it mentally, or you will not have the total concentration that you need for the remainder of your test. You can still gain good results even with an error, but if you compound that single mistake with further errors because you were not attentive to your riding, you will find your marks tumbling down.

Allowing yourself to dwell on any form of error has several possible unfortunate results:

- You may take the wrong course because, with too many things on your mind, you can forget where you are going.

- You may ride badly, not giving your horse enough preparation time or clear enough aiding to help him manage the rest of the test with ease.

- You may become *disempowered*. When you make an error, your mind tells your body that it can't do the job. Your body believes what your mind tells it, your body tone collapses and you slump forward and become weak, which results in a cessation of effectiveness, thus confirming that your mind was absolutely right – you really *can't* ride this test!

- Taking your attention away from your horse can cause him to lose confidence, at best resulting in loss of attention to you and, at worst, giving him licence to spook or misbehave.

We all make mistakes, no matter how experienced we are but once an error has occurred, you need to put it behind you, or shelve it somewhere in your mind to look at *after* the test has finished. This is easier said than done, but with conscious effort and practice you *will* be able to do it.

Part Two

Competing

8 General Competing Techniques

This part of the book takes a close look at how to ride movements from dressage tests, how to correct them when they start to go wrong, and how to prevent them from going wrong the next time.

What it will *not* do is to discuss in detail how to correct the *training* of these issues: for detailed information on correct training and training corrections please see my previous book, *The Building Blocks of Training* (J. A. Allen, 2008).

> **Warning**
> It is important that you are also always aware that any evasions your horse might exhibit *may* be due to undiagnosed physical issues such as a sore back, low-grade lameness, saddle fitting or teeth and bitting problems. Such issues should, of course, always be dealt with as a priority. This warning will not be repeated in the TROUBLESHOOTING sections of subsequent chapters but should always be kept in mind.

You should also remember that **quality** is always more important than **accuracy**. This is because the dressage judge is primarily judging your horse's *way of going*, with accuracy only becoming a factor if inaccurate riding is avoiding the difficulty of the movement, e.g. riding too large a circle because riding the correct smaller size would show up a problem.

To reiterate: **ride the horse, not the test.**

Test Advice

Learn Your Test Correctly

Learning a test is not just about memorising the prescribed sequence of movements; it is also about understanding the geometry of the arena so that you can place the movements correctly, and understand how to use one movement to prepare for the next.

Geometry of the dressage arena

You may find that you have misconceptions about the layout of the arena unless you have looked closely at the precise placement of the markers. Take a look at the measurements for the markers on the diagram below: the so-called 'quarter markers' F, K, H and M are 6 m from the corners not, as their names might suggest (at least in the 40 m arena), 10 m, and in the 60 m long arena, the extra letters R, S, V and P are 18 m from the corners not, as you might expect, 20 m.

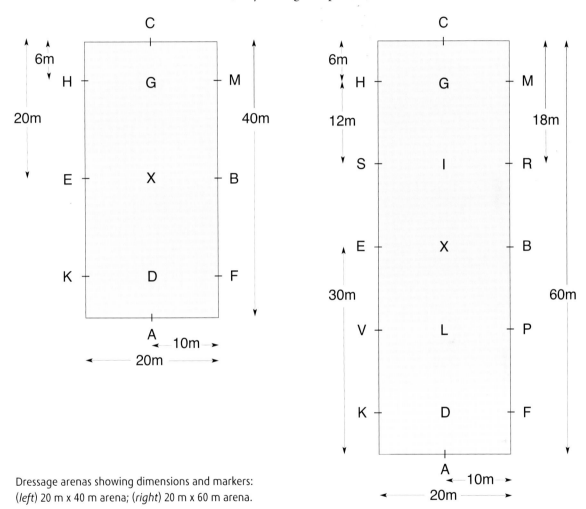

Dressage arenas showing dimensions and markers:
(*left*) 20 m x 40 m arena; (*right*) 20 m x 60 m arena.

Figure Riding

If you are starting with erroneous assumptions about the placing of the markers, it will be little wonder that your figure riding will be less than acceptable to a judge! Look at the diagrams showing simple 20 m circles in the 60 m arena. The diagram on the left shows how an inexperienced rider might ride what they consider to be 20 m circles at each end of the arena and in its centre, whilst the diagram on the right shows the correctly shaped figures that a more experienced rider will produce.

20 m circles in the 60 m arena – incorrect (*left*) and correct (*right*) shapes.

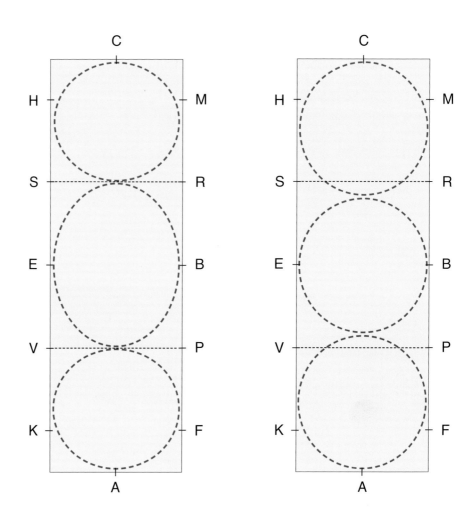

These differences arise because the less experienced competitor will tend to mentally divide the arena into imaginary squares defined by the markers and ride circles within these boundaries. However, as you can see from the diagram with marked distances, these are not true squares, and lead to circles that are squashed (egg-shaped or oval) at the two ends, and over-large in the centre of the arena.

Improve your spatial awareness

Two ways in which you can improve your *spatial awareness* of the true sizes and shapes of these figures are:

1. Repetitively drawing the shapes on a diagram of the arena. You can purchase ready-designed whiteboards that allow you to erase and use again, or photocopy some templates that you have measured and drawn yourself.

2. Carefully and precisely mark out several points of your chosen figure (e.g. a 20 m circle) in your arena using markers such as cones (soft and easily knocked over if you inadvertently touch them) and practise riding around them. This will give you a good idea of how a shape should *feel* in terms of how much you need to turn your body and consequently how much bend your horse should have for a particular size of circle. Experienced riders ride test movements from a memory template of how each shape should feel – this is a good way to start building up your own catalogue of feel templates.

Practising a 10 m circle at B: Tracey and Zevs are riding just inside the carefully positioned markers to get a feel for the correct size and shape of the figure.

As each movement is described in subsequent chapters you will find it accompanied by a diagram of the correct layout relative to the markers for you to add to your collection.

Riding movements 'at' the marker

The correct moment to ride a movement or transition at a specific marker is as *the rider's body* is directly above (or in front of) the marker: not the horse's nose, shoulders or tail, but *your* body.

To achieve this with precision means that you must *prepare*, i.e. warn your horse, at least two strides *before* you reach the marker; it will take his body this long to respond to your aids. Remember, signals have to pass to his brain, be recognised, and then send instructions to his limbs, all of which takes time. With some horses, especially youngsters, this can take quite a number of strides and you need to find out by experimentation at home just how many strides before a marker you need to start preparing, bearing in mind that at a show he may take even longer to respond because his attention may not be fully on you.

This is especially important with downward transitions when it will take him longer to get his body organised to make the transition in a correct manner, by taking weight back onto his hind legs, than it will to do it incorrectly, by bracing a front leg, and not only do you not want to show an incorrect technique to the judge, you don't want to teach him that such a thing is acceptable in the arena or he will believe that he can do it that way again. I repeat, take the time to *prepare*.

If, when you approach a marker, you know that you are not going to be able to perform a transition at precisely the correct moment if, for example, your horse is becoming tense with anticipation, or you will be in the wrong moment in his stride, then doing it early is better than doing it late – the judge is more likely to forgive a slightly early transition, but will almost always penalise a late one.

Riding movements 'to' a marker

When you ride a line towards a marker, such as a diagonal of the school, e.g. 'HXF change the rein', always aim for a point on the track around 2 m *before* the marker; your goal is to have the horse's whole body fully on the track just as *your* body passes the marker.

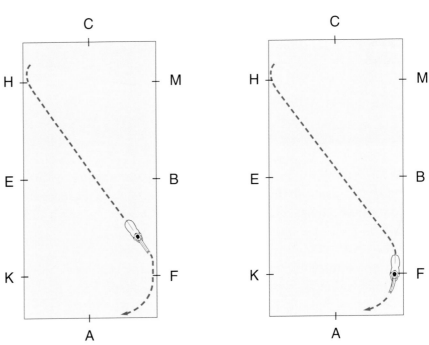

Changing the rein on the diagonal HXF: (*left*) Aim to meet the track about 2 m before F; (*right*) By the time the horse's whole body is on the track, your shoulders will be level with F.

Horses are notorious for drifting sideways, especially in the early days of their training, so know in which direction your individual habitually drifts and adjust your aim accordingly. In the example above (changing direction from the left rein to the right rein across the diagonal), if he tends to drift towards the left he will automatically take you to the track a few metres early and you must ensure that it is not *too* early. If he drifts habitually to the right, you must really focus on your goal of 2 m before F or you will find yourself without the space to ride into the following corner.

If your test also requires a transition at the end of the diagonal, e.g. 'BMCH working canter; HXF change rein; F working trot', aim to ride the transition as his nose comes to the track; this will give you sufficient time to organise him for the corner.

Ride your corners

Corners are in general poorly, or at best indifferently, ridden and as such are a wasted resource: **every corner is an opportunity to improve balance and engagement, and to set up your next movement.**

Here again we must look at the geometry of the arena to truly understand how to ride corners. You may ride in an arena that has developed a 'track', i.e. a deep groove in the surface that everyone follows because it is around the perimeter of the arena and it takes effort to leave it. Because the most frequently repeated movement in schooling is the 20 m circle, most often each end of the school is defined by a track that is actually one half of a 20 m circle, *not* by two corners joined by a short straight line as it should be.

With a young horse it is absolutely correct not to ride too deeply into the corners because he has neither the balance nor the suppleness to achieve this with ease. However, by the time that he is capable of performing even the easiest of competitive tests he should be able to travel around the short side showing distinct, if not yet deep, corners.

Every corner should be ridden as one quarter of a circle – the size of the circle depending upon his level of training (10 m in the earlier stages and ultimately 6 m for the advanced horse) – linked by a straight section as you pass A or C. Clearly the shallower your corner the shorter your straight line will be, but it should still be distinct from the bend in your corners.

Your goals for the corner are that he:

- Maintains the rhythm and quality of his gait.

- Remains upright (not leaning to either side) with a clear inside bend and genuine alignment to the arc of the curve.

(*Left*) An incorrect corner following the arc of the circle; (*right*) a true corner.

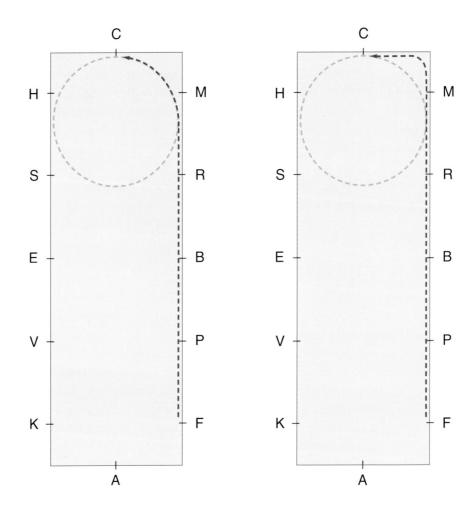

As you approach each corner, especially the first one of a short side, make a half-halt to improve his balance before you enter the corner. For how to ride a half-halt, see my book *The Building Blocks of Training* (J. A. Allen, 2008). You can also use half-halts *during* both corners – possibly more than once in each – to achieve maximum engagement before you leave the short side, this is especially useful if your next movement is, for example, medium trot.

To understand *why* corners can help you to gain impulsion and engagement, watch a supple horse travelling around a curve (circle, corner etc.) and notice that his inside hind leg steps further forward (i.e. is more engaged) than his outside hind: this is simply due to the geometry of the figure and his alignment to it – see the diagram on page 111.

Riding well into the corner with clear inside bend; you can see the engaging effect in the well-bent joints of the inside hind leg as it travels forward. The author riding Lover Boy, also known as Stanley.

Note

A horse may swing his quarters outward to avoid this engaging effect, especially if he is stiff in either the hind leg joints or laterally, to the bend. Achieving correct alignment of his body is your first goal.

If you simply coast around corners he may well slow down rather than make the extra effort needed to maintain his tempo. If, on the other hand, you use stronger, but not quicker, leg aids as you travel through the corner you will come out of it at the same speed but with his hind legs more engaged beneath him: the perfect use of a corner to prepare your next movement.

Riding Transitions

Prior to transitions always try to have your horse working in the best balance and quality of gait possible. Make a conscious effort also to sit as well as you can before asking for any transition. These factors will affect how good the transition is and, as a result, the quality of the work *after* the transition. A poor transition will result in poor balance and poor quality of subsequent movements.

Give him adequate warning that you are about to ask for a transition. If you suddenly realise that you are at the required marker for a transition, it is too late: he cannot respond instantly and trying to ask him to do so will make him anxious, causing stiffening, a poor transition and subsequent tension because he has been rattled both by your unreasonable demand and his inability to comply. You *must plan ahead* for every transition, starting your preparation (which is also his warning) at least three strides *before* the marker, and with some horses as many as five strides before. Know your own horse's response time.

Transitions should, above all, be fluent. At the early levels, progressive transitions can still earn high marks, but to earn a higher mark from Elementary level upwards they must be both fluent and direct.

Upward transitions

Upward transitions should be crisp to the aid, i.e. a horse should spring into the next gait without hesitation as a result of a light, discreet aid. If you have to ask more than once, then he is not responsive enough and you should work on this at home.

At a show, both tension and lack of attention can cause his responses to differ from their norm: from explosive at one end of the scale, to totally ignoring your aids at the other. After a few outings you should know your horse well enough to be able to predict his responses – both level of response and response time – and adjust your preparation time and aiding accordingly. Clearly you want him to start reacting at a show in the same manner as he does at home, but this may take time to achieve and in the short term you should use the aids that you know will gain the best response and so, the best marks.

As mentioned earlier, you can go part way towards addressing a lazy response during the warm-up. An over-sharp response is not so simply dealt with and is best improved by working on general relaxation rather than practising the transition and potentially adding to his tension.

When preparing for **canter transitions**, take great care in your preparation to:

- Have him correctly bent.

- Have him in a balanced, steady, i.e. *not* hurried, and impulsive gait prior to asking.

- Give a clear half-halt as a warning before applying your aids.

- Remain sitting up, not leaning forward where you will put your weight over his shoulders.

- Maintain your contact so that he does not run into canter.

In all the early tests, canter transitions are asked for on a curve, either on a circle or in a corner, so that the correct canter lead should be easy to achieve as long as your training, preparation and aids are clear.

Direct transitions from walk to canter should be clearly direct, i.e. without trot steps, unless the test sheet says otherwise: e.g. 'transition may be progressive'.

Downward transitions

Downward transitions are often the most poorly ridden moves in the earlier-level tests, probably owing to a lack of understanding of what constitutes a good downward transition and how to ride one!

In a good downward transition your horse should:

1. Gradually bring his hind legs a little further beneath his body during the preceding three strides, showing a visible lowering of his haunches.

2. Make the change of gait with no alteration in his outline.

3. Move without hesitation from clear steps of one gait into clear steps of the next gait without any shuffling or running steps, and with no loss of impulsion or forwardness.

4. He should accept the contact with a soft, relaxed jaw and with no stiffening of his back or frame.

The greatest factor (apart from training) in achieving transitions that conform to this ideal is *preparation*. Springing an unexpected transition upon him will force him to compromise at least some if not all of these requirements; he must have warning and that means preparing for any transition *at least* three strides before the place where the transition is to be performed. (For detailed descriptions of how to ride correct transitions see *The Building Blocks of Training* [J. A. Allen, 2008].)

Combining transitions with movements
Examples

'A working canter left; A circle left 15 m.' and 'C halt and rein-back one horse's length; proceed collected trot; C circle right 15 m and on returning to C collected canter right.'

To ride movements such as these requires that you give both transition aids and turning aids *at the same time*. In other words, do not give your transition aid first, and then think about turning, or you will overshoot the start of your circle.

Correcting Your Position during a Test

If you know that your body is likely to lose its correct position during a test, e.g. become crooked, or you have legs that rise up the saddle flaps, take a moment to adjust your position during the free walk. Here you have the opportunity to rearrange your seat and legs while he is walking. Lift your legs clear of the saddle and circle them backward, turning your heels outward so that your leg comes back onto the saddle with your toes and knees pointing forward, and your legs stretched fully down. Watch advanced riders; you will see many of them do just this. This adjustment will help your seat to be as straight and deep as possible before you continue with the test.

Shrug your shoulders back and down as well, and draw your body up taller. As a result, when you make the transition out of walk, you will be in the best posture that you can achieve, which can only assist your riding of the remainder of the test.

Of course, this can only be done easily if your horse is relaxed in free walk. With a tense horse you may need to sit as quietly as possible, with any movement likely to cause him to jog, but experiment a time or two and see what happens.

Shortening the Reins

Your reins should always be shortened in such a way that you never lose your contact. This means not wriggling your fingers along the reins which, as you do not have your fingers closed during this process, has the potential for you to either drop the rein entirely or to have it removed from your hand by your horse. It also gives a meaningless vibration, i.e. an aid, to your horse's mouth.

1. Bridge your reins into one hand. This is done by turning both your hands flat with your palms facing downward and then taking hold of both reins in one hand, and letting go with the other. See how the reins are positioned in my left hand in the first photograph opposite, with each rein coming out of the opposite side of my fist.

2. Whilst holding the reins in one hand, move the other hand further along the reins towards your horse's mouth.

3. Now bridge both reins into the hand that you have already moved and repeat the process, moving the other hand along the reins to a matching position.

4. Release the reins back into both hands.

Handling a Schooling Whip during a Test

The rules of some competitions, especially championship classes, do not allow a whip to be carried (check your rule book), but if it is permitted you should make a decision: do you really need to carry a whip?

(*Left*) Shortening first the right rein and (*right*) then the left.

If you are unlikely to use a whip during the test – either because you rarely use it anyway, or because it might cause an adverse reaction such as kicking out – then consider riding without. Not carrying a whip is the simplest option, and good practice for when you ride in those tests where one is not permitted.

If you feel that you must carry it, then you need to consider when and where you will change it from one side to the other, or if you will ride with it in one hand throughout. The latter is less advisable as horses tend to move away from whichever side the whip is carried, and so carrying it on the outside during a test may, with some horses, lead to straightness issues. If, however, you have a horse who is only difficult about going away from one of your legs, you may sensibly choose this option.

Riding indoors is usually a good case for changing the whip to the inside every time that you change the rein, as it may scrape along the wall and possibly startle your horse.

Unless you have elected to keep the whip in one hand throughout, map out during practice exactly when you will change it over. For example:

- If changing the whip disturbs your horse or makes him anxious you may want to change it over just prior to changing the rein in free walk, or just after, as opposed to during the walk, otherwise you may cause him to jog.

- Try not to change it as you are approaching a transition. If you get your reins in a tangle, or he becomes tense, it will likely not go well.

- *Read* your test carefully to see where the marks are given, and try not to change it where there is a possibility of affecting two movements.

- Make a decision before you start about which side you will carry the whip when you enter the arena; this is usually determined by which direction you will turn at C, unless your test starts with a change of rein.

- Review handling the whip during the salute (see page 108). Even if you have no halt on entry, you will always have a finishing halt.

Changing a schooling whip

1. Bridge your reins (see description on page 92) into the hand that is holding the whip so that you have everything in the one hand.

2. Lift the empty hand and reach over beyond the hand that is holding the reins and whip.

3. Turn the free hand so that the knuckles are towards your body.

4. Take hold of the whip with the free hand, below the hand holding the reins.

5. Open the thumb of the hand holding the reins to release the whip.

6. In a smooth but unhurried motion, turn the whip upright so that it passes in front of your face (*not* allowing it to droop forward where it might touch your horse's ears) and on down until it finishes in the normal position in which it is carried, now on the new side.

7. Retake the reins in both hands. You may find it helpful to link the top of the whip into the thumb of the hand that is holding the reins while you separate them back into both hands, then take hold of it in the normal position.

Steps versus Strides

Some tests ask for a specified number of steps of a gait, for example: 'Over A transition to walk (2-5 steps) and then working trot'.

A 'step' is the movement of one foreleg, whereas a 'stride' is one complete sequence of legs in a particular gait. To count steps, simply count each front footfall.

Changing Diagonals during a Test

Try always to be on the correct diagonal for your direction of travel during your tests: being on the wrong diagonal can interfere with your body position, making your hips twist towards the outside. This can cause problems with your horse's bend as your

a)

b)

c)

d)

a) Hold the reins and whip in one hand. b) Take hold of the whip with your free hand. c) Turn the whip over, keeping it upright so that you are in no danger of clipping your horse's ears!
d) Hold the whip linked into your thumb whilst you retake the reins into both hands.

weight will be in the wrong place and your legs may be pulled out of position. The knock-on effect of this can be to make him tense as he tries to sort out what you intend.

You may have been taught that when you change the rein you should change the diagonal as you pass over X, but this is not ideal unless you are going from one curve to another, i.e. from a half-circle in one direction to a half-circle in the opposite direction. Changing your diagonal has the potential to cause a loss of balance and/or rhythm, especially if you are also performing lengthened strides. If you are travelling on a straight line, therefore (across a diagonal of the school, up the centre line, or on an incline back to the track), change your diagonal either *at the beginning* of your line, or else leave it until two to three strides before you reach the track. Do not leave it any later than this, as your horse must have time to respond by changing his body bend to the new direction.

Rising or Sitting Trot?

In most of the earlier-level tests you can make a choice about whether to perform your test in either rising or sitting trot unless otherwise stated by the rules governing your competition; again, always check the appropriate rule book.

Assuming that the choice is yours to make, you are also free to change from one to the other *during* your test, even during a movement. You do not have to pick one and then stick to it.

You may find that your horse will perform certain movements better in sitting trot than in rising trot, and vice versa, so choose accordingly. You may also make the choice to try sitting trot, and then find that he doesn't feel forward enough, which is a good case for changing your mind during the test and going rising. You may also need to change from rising to sitting trot in certain areas of the arena if he is being spooky: sitting can be more effective and may be safer!

Be sensible with your decision: if your sitting trot seat is not yet good, then keep on rising until your technique has improved.

Taking the Wrong Course

No matter how well you learn your tests, at some point in your career you will take a wrong course – we have *all* done it. The important thing when it happens is to not let it upset you.

1. **When the bell rings, stop** and either look at the judge or, if they are too far away, ride towards their car/box.

2. The judge will check with you that you understand what you did wrong and where you should be going next, and will tell you where they want you to restart the test. *Do not* take your instruction from your reader.

3. When you restart your test, allow yourself as much room as you can (without overdoing it) to re-establish the appropriate gait in a relaxed rhythm *before* you reach the point where the judge will restart marking. If you rush back into the test you may mess up the next movement or two by being flustered or having a tense horse.

4. Forget your error. This is tough to do but is one of the presentation skills that you must foster; many people have still won a class despite an error of course. Focus on riding what still lies ahead of you; if your focus is centred on your mistake, you will not give full attention to your horse and he *will* notice, reacting according to his temperament with either anxiety or cheek.

Error of course or error of test?

An 'error of course' is the technical term for taking the wrong course, whilst an 'error of test' is, for example, when you fail to take your reins in one hand at the salute, or rise to the trot when you should be sitting. In such cases it is up to the judge to either ring the bell and restart you onto the right course (essential when you have missed a movement or turned the wrong way), or to simply mark on your sheet where the error occurred, but not to stop you if it would interrupt the flow of the test. In both cases there will be a deduction of marks.

If you perform a movement slightly wrongly, starting it at the wrong marker for example, when that movement is to be repeated on the other rein, the judge *should* stop you the first time and correct the error because you may do it in the other direction as well and gain another error penalty. That decision, however, is down to the individual judge, and judges (contrary to what some people believe), are only human, so they may not make the decision you would have preferred.

Using Your Voice

Remember *not* to use your voice once you enter the arena or else you risk having marks deducted, and this includes clicking with your tongue. Many of us do this habitually when riding, often without realising we are doing it. If in doubt, keep your mouth shut!

Dealing with Spooking

Many factors are involved in dealing with spooky horses, some of which have already been discussed earlier in Chapter 2. Indeed, whole books exist on the subject, so the advice here relates merely to handling the odd spook that a horse might offer within the competition arena, rather than an in-depth dissertation on the approach to spooking in general.

1. Turn his face slightly *away* from the object of his concern; do not try to make him 'look at it'. Use an indirect inside rein: take your inside hand inward towards or even slightly across his withers, to push his shoulders *towards* the problem area. See the photograph on page 219 for how this hand position should look. Bear in mind that this picture is of counter-canter, and when using this technique for dealing with spooking you will need to take both of your hands towards the *outside* of the arena, not the inside as you do when turning in counter-canter.

2. This positioning may be just a slight lateral flexion at the poll (and as brief as one stride), or a full shoulder-in position – use whatever is effective – and *ride him forward*.

3. Use a strong inside leg: feel like you are trying to leg-yield outward to prevent him from leaving the track and keep him going forward.

4. Use your inside rein influence for *as short a time as possible*; if you are too strong with the rein for too long, you may increase his anxiety and/or resistance.

5. Unless you feel him becoming tense, the next time you approach the same part of the arena, act as if you expect nothing to happen – it is quite likely that if you dealt with it firmly but sympathetically the first time, nothing will.

Collection

Collected gaits first appear in Elementary-level tests. Collection can be defined as: 'increased engagement and activity of the hind legs with supple and bent joints, stepping forward under the body to result in lowering of the haunches'.

In these earlier tests, the *degree* of collection expected by the judge *is only sufficient to enable your horse to perform the movements of the test with ease*. In other words, don't panic and put the brakes on!

When faced with the directive to show 'collected' gaits, many people react by tightening their contact and restricting the steps; this is *not* what the judge wants to see.

Collection should come about as a gradual development of your horse's increasing strength, suppleness and straightness, i.e. as a result of correct schooling. If you have followed the advice already set out earlier in this book, you will not be competing in a test with movements that your horse finds difficult to perform, so you will already have him sufficiently 'collected' to find the movements easy.

The best way to handle collection as asked for at this earliest stage is to ride the test using the gait (in terms of impulsion and tempo) that you use when schooling at home. When the test then asks for working gaits, ride more positively forward for greater ground coverage. Leave yourself with enough in reserve to still show yet a greater difference for your medium gaits: you can ride these at the longest ground coverage that you can achieve at this stage of his training, as extended gaits are not yet required.

Be sure to show clear 'gear changes' when required to move from one variation of gait to the next, but *never* try to shorten his strides artificially using your reins – collect him using half-halts, bearing in mind that a half-halt is a brief application of combined driving and restraining aids, and is completed by a softening of your contact to allow forwardness.

TROUBLESHOOTING

'Losing balance in corner'; 'leaning over in corners'; 'speeds up in corners'

Review your riding of corners in training: correcting any of these issues in competition is dependent upon correcting:

1. His habit.

2. His responses.

If you permit him to perform his corners poorly at home, probably due to a simple lack of attention to the manner in which he performs them, you cannot expect him to do them correctly in the competition arena.

'Wrong bend in corners'

This is most likely to occur when you are travelling around the arena on your horse's stiffer rein, or alternatively it may be as a result of spooking. It may simply be that you are leaving him to his own devices and his natural crookedness is asserting itself.

Check that you are *asking* him for bend in the corners by applying your inside calf against his ribcage to ask him to contract his ribcage muscles on that side. Use also a small vibration on your inside rein to ask him to turn his head towards the inside – this is particularly important if spooking is an issue because you need him to look *away* from whatever he is spooking at, not to look *at* it.

If you still find it difficult to produce inside bend from him in the corners there are two exercises that you need to do at home:

1. Ride a small circle in *every* corner of your school; the size is dependant upon how supple your horse is but do not make it smaller than he can manage with relative

ease. Do this whenever you ride large around your school until he anticipates the circle and starts to bend around to the inside as you approach each corner. Once this is established, go back to riding around the school normally, but anytime that he tries to go around a corner without inside bend, immediately put a circle into that corner. Clearly you cannot do this in a test, but establishing the habit at home will carry over into his general way of going wherever you are.

2. Establish leg-yielding, and then if he pushes against your inside leg, i.e. refuses to bend, as you approach a corner, simply leg-yield outward *throughout* the corner. You can do this also in the competition arena – it is simply a matter of gaining obedience to your inside leg.

'Not using/riding into corners'

When you first start test riding there is an awful lot to think about and staying out on the track, especially through the corners, is just one item amongst many that demand your attention.

If your horse lacks bend and balance, falling inward away from the track/corners will just tend to happen all on its own, especially in canter work. If this comment appears on your sheets, work on it at home where you can give it more attention; indeed, work on it as the main focus of your attention for a time or two by riding through a test pattern and insisting that your horse stays out on the track and uses the whole arena.

See also the section on page 87 about riding corners as distinct from riding half a 20 m circle at the short side of the arena.

You drop your whip during the test

If you drop your whip, you must carry on without it; you will neither be permitted to dismount to retrieve it, nor to have it handed back up to you, but make sure someone picks it up after your test is completed.

'Not enough steps shown'

Did you start to count *before* he was truly established in the new gait? This is particularly relevant to walk steps; he must be in a clear four-beat walk sequence before you start counting; jogging steps do not count, so wait until he steps out in a clear sequence even if this takes time to become established.

'Lacks collection'; 'needs more collection'; 'show collection more clearly'

You are unlikely to see these comments in the earlier-level tests but if they do appear it means that you did not show a clear enough *difference* between your collected and working gaits, and vice versa. Next time you compete try to show a clearer transition from one to the other but *do not* try to achieve more 'collection' by restricting his strides to a smaller size. (Review the sections above, on achieving the required degree of collection for the earlier-level tests, page 98.)

Transitions

Problems with transitions are most likely to be:

- Rider error, e.g. your aids are insufficiently clear or correct under the pressure of competition. Try to clearly establish your aiding at home so that you do not have to think about it in competition.

- Lack of preparation – you failed to give him enough time to respond to your aids. Think and plan further ahead.

- Training issues such as his responses being either too slow or too tense – more homework needed.

9 The Entry

A Good First Impression

The judge may be so busy writing comments for the previous competitor that this will be the first time she actually looks at you. Now is your chance to make a great first impression with an impressive entry that sets the tone for the rest of your test. You should have decided from which rein you will enter during practice at home before you ever get anywhere near to the competition arena. Of course there will always be occasions when you have to revise your choice as a result of arena layout, but in general you should try to stick to your decision.

If you are entering from outside the arena and the A marker is set back, try to give yourself as much room as possible to get straight before you set foot inside the arena. Keep the A marker on the outside of your turn and ride as close to it as you can; do not go around the marker as this involves making bend and directional changes which, this close to the arena entrance, will almost certainly compromise his balance and straightness, so affecting your centre line.

Centre Line without Halt

In the early tests you do not have to halt on your entry centre line, however there are still a number of features that you must take care of:

- Outline.

- Straightness.

- Rhythm and tempo.

- A fluent turn at C.

Outline   Try to ensure that your horse is in as good an outline as you can produce *before* you enter the arena. Make the most of your time before the bell goes and use your turn onto the centre line to help bring his hind legs underneath his body and to maintain his outline. Once you are *on* the centre line try to avoid doing anything

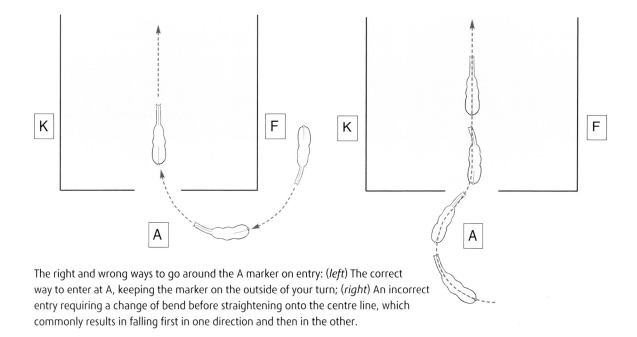

The right and wrong ways to go around the A marker on entry: (*left*) The correct way to enter at A, keeping the marker on the outside of your turn; (*right*) An incorrect entry requiring a change of bend before straightening onto the centre line, which commonly results in falling first in one direction and then in the other.

obvious about his outline: one of the most disappointing sights that a judge sees is the first centre line marred by a rider frantically swinging their horse's head from side to side as they try to get him 'on the bit'. Far better to leave his outline alone once you are committed to the centre line; in fact, it is quite hard for a judge to really see exactly how round a horse is from the head-on view, unless he is a long way above the bit, and many will give the benefit of the doubt, so once committed – leave his outline alone.

Straightness   As you turn onto the centre line fix your eyes on C, keep the marker directly between your horse's ears, and ride straight at it! The more positively forward you ride, the straighter your centre line will be. Having said that, do be careful not to push him out of his natural **rhythm and tempo**: riding positively forward does not mean rushing him, which would compromise his balance. If he does lose straightness, do *not* try to correct it by attempting to realign him, just keep your eyes on your goal and ride forward towards it; this will straighten him more effectively than correction. (See Troubleshooting on page 110.)

A fluent turn at C depends on good preparation. Take, for example, 'C track right'.

1. As you approach G, start to put a little more weight into your right stirrup.

2. At the same time, squeeze a little more strongly with your right lower leg to start him bending to the right and lightly vibrate the right rein with your fingers (a quick movement of just the fingers, not the entire hand) to ask for flexion

(turning at the poll) towards the right. Keep your left rein snug against his neck so that he does not bulge out through his left shoulder.

3. Turn your upper body to the right as you pass over **G**, bringing *both* of your hands to the right. Take care not to lean over to the side.

4. Ride actively forward with your inside leg around the turn; this is a relatively tight arc, and unless you ask for more impulsion than you would on a straight line, he may slow down.

5. Think of the turn as a half 10 m circle and as you finish it, turn your shoulders towards where you are going next, either straight along the track or across the diagonal.

Centre Line with Halt

To produce a good, straight, and hopefully square, halt at X in addition to the other features described above, you must learn to ride *forward* into your halts. The biggest mistake that you can make with a halt is to 'put the brakes on': this will invariably result in resistance and/or crookedness, and in addition will put him on his forehand, which will make your move-off harder.

The effect of too much hand on the halt: on the forehand and crooked. Nikki and Leo's Orlando (Ollie) showing how not to do it!

In the earlier-level tests, transitions to halt are allowed to be progressive through a few walk steps (preferably two, or at most three). By Elementary/Medium level your halts should be almost direct with no intervening walk steps, although it is always better to produce a good halt without resistance than to be over-demanding about directness at the expense of maintaining a soft contact and relaxed outline.

To make a direct transition requires that your horse is supple enough over his back and in his hind leg joints to enable him to step underneath his body with ease, is strong enough in the haunches to carry more weight behind, and clearly understands your aids so that he has no reason to resist.

At the higher levels the entry may be in canter rather than trot, requiring sophisticated levels of straightness and strength, and is beyond the scope of this book.

A good halt is made up of a number of different components, which can be listed in order of priority as:

1. Immobile.

2. A good outline.

3. Attentive.

4. Straight.

5. Square.

6. Engaged.

To produce a good halt at X:

1. First, make sure that you know where X is! This might sound daft, but very many marks are lost by riders halting too early or too late. As you approach the centre of the school, flick your eyes to the sides to locate E and B (*do not* move your head from side to side as this may affect his balance and straightness), then estimate (this will take practice) how many steps you are away from X.

2. Begin your preparation three to five steps before X. You should know from practice how many steps of preparation he is likely to need before coming to a full halt; a lazy horse will need less than a very forward horse.

3. Take sitting trot and move both your legs slightly back, closing your calves softly onto his sides to ask him to step under his body with his hind legs.

4. Hold your upper body and seat *still* to ask for the transition; do *not* pull on the reins. Keep your eyes fixed on C to stay straight.

5. If he stiffens or tries to hollow, vibrate both reins with your fingers, but do not move your hands backward.

6. Close your thighs more firmly around the saddle – not enough to grip, but enough to hold the saddle still.

7. Maintain these resisting aids until he comes to the halt. Your contact should be consistent and stay still and soft throughout, with no movement backwards from your hands (finger-produced vibrations do not involve moving your whole hand). This will encourage him to step up to the bridle and produce an

engaged and hopefully square halt depending on his level of training (see Chapter 23 for requirements for the halt at the different levels). Too strong a rein aid will make him stiffen and he may stop himself by bracing a front leg, or by hollowing and so stiffening his back, leaving his hind legs parked out behind. Strong hands may also result in him swinging his haunches to one side, as his front end stops before his hind end, producing a crooked halt.

Immobility

The first and most important feature of a halt is that it is immobile: **immobility** means there must be no movement of your horse's legs, feet or head. A switching tail is not a problem, so long as it is not as a result of tension. Try to remain relaxed yourself: any tension in your body will make your horse anxious and so likely to fidget. Keep your contact consistent – so that he does not move forward – and your legs lightly closed around him – so that he doesn't move back – but be soft and sympathetic with these controls or he may feel trapped and panic.

As in all things equestrian, you are dealing with an interactive system in which one thing affects another. In this case, the horse that is attentive and in a round outline will stand still more easily than one who is above the bit and sightseeing.

A straight halt. Head on, only his front feet are visible to the judge.

If you arrive at a halt that you are less than satisfied with because it is perhaps slightly crooked, or with at least one leg out of square, do *not* try to correct it after you have stopped; **leave it alone!** The more you fiddle, the worse it is likely to become, and the more your marks will drop. Once you are in halt, however positioned, **stand still.** The exception to this rule is when the horse is above the bit, which can be dealt with without requiring him to move any feet. (Correcting the halt is possible on a more highly trained horse, but that is beyond the levels dealt with in this book.)

If at all possible, try to have him *straight*: the judge will only be able to see his front feet, so being square behind is unnecessary. Of course if he leaves a hind leg very far behind, he will appear unbalanced (listing to one side) and that *can* be seen, but if he is ridden correctly forward into the halt this should not happen.

The salute

Your next challenge will be to make your salute without losing your immobility as any shifting of your weight or alteration of your contact could be potential reasons for him to move.

Once you are absolutely certain that he is standing still, take your reins carefully into your left hand. This involves 'bridging' the reins: see page 92 for a description of how to do this with the accompanying photographs. Next:

1. Remove your right hand and drop it down behind your right thigh with your palm turned in, towards your horse's flank; d*o not* swing your hand out to the side with a flourish.

2. Drop your head forward from your neck for a second or two. *Do not* curl your shoulders or your whole upper body forward, just your head. The movement should be smooth, but quite crisp.

(*Left*) The correct way to nod your head to the judge. (*Right*) An incorrect salute: Maggie on Seven demonstrating how not to do it by bowing from the waist.

3. If you are a man, you should check the current rule book regarding the requirement or otherwise for you to remove your hat during a salute. If you *are* going to remove your hat, hold it with the lining facing your leg, or to the rear, *don't* show it to the judge!

4. Lift your head.

5. Bring your right hand back up to the reins and separate them into your two hands.

Handling the whip during the salute

You have three options here:

1. Approach the halt with the whip in your left hand. Take care whilst transferring both reins into your left hand not to wave it around and startle him.

2. If the whip is in your right hand (because you will need it on that side after you move off), you can link it into your left thumb along with the reins.

Hold the whip linked into your left thumb.

3. There is no written requirement to salute with your right hand although it is customary. If your whip is in your right hand you can choose to salute by putting your reins (and whip) into your right hand and dropping your left.

On no account keep your whip in the hand that you lower. Not only might you touch him inadvertently and startle him, but this is also an incorrect salute that the judge will comment upon and may also choose to penalise you for with a deduction of marks. The rules are not firm on this point, but the judge would be within her rights to consider this an error, resulting in a two-mark deduction.

Saluting with the left hand dropped. Mary on Bertie.

An incorrect salute with the whip held in the lowered hand.

Do not forget to salute! This fault is more often seen at the end of a test, when you may be so pleased with your horse that you forget to salute in your enthusiasm for patting and praising him, or when a test has been a difficult experience and you want to leave the arena as fast as possible, but you may also forget at the start when you are so focussed on riding the test ahead of you. As with keeping the whip in your hand when you salute, forgetting to salute altogether can also earn mark deductions.

The move-off

If your preparatory training has been good enough your horse should be capable of making a direct transition from halt to trot, and this is your goal for the move-off. Not only does it show willingness and a degree of impulsion, it will also help you to keep him straight for the remainder of your centre line. If he dribbles forward in walk he will be far more likely to have his weight on his forehand and lose his balance towards his favourite shoulder – the one that he leans on as a result of his natural crookedness – resulting in him falling off the centre line.

Whilst trying not to startle him with too sudden an aid, ask him to move off at

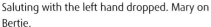

trot with a clear and equal closure of both your lower legs together with a feeling of springing upward with your pelvis, which should not make you jump out of the saddle, but rather simulate the feel of your flexible lower back and swinging seat in sitting trot: almost a feeling of sucking the saddle upward. If he is prone to coming above the bit in the move-off, use small soft vibrations equally on both reins to ask him to remain relaxed in his jaw and poll as you ask him to trot. As he moves off, relax your contact sufficiently that he can move freely forward with confidence and purpose.

Once you are into trot, continue to ride straight towards C, and finally, ride a fluent turn at C as described on pages 103–4.

TROUBLESHOOTING

'Wobbled on centre line'; 'centre line could have been straighter'

Review the instructions above for how to approach and ride the centre line.

- Making a good turn into the arena at A is the basis of a straight centre line so that you don't have any corrections to make at the beginning.

- Keeping your eyes fixed on the C marker and riding positively forward towards it is also fundamental to maintaining straightness.

- If a wobble does occur, **do not** try to correct it: this will only result in a fishtailing effect, where you swing from one correction to the next. Instead, once you have left your intended line, simply realign things so that you are once again looking at C centrally between your horse's ears and go for it! Positive forward riding is the only correction needed to straighten out a centre line.

- Wobbles on the centre line can be a result of loss of attention; if he is looking at something that has caught his eye, his body will follow his line of sight, so try to keep him looking at C.

- If your problem is that he is *backing off* from C (perhaps he doesn't like the look of the judge's car), your answer is to ride *really positively forward*, with strong legs and even your stick if you need to.

- His natural crookedness can be a problem here, especially if he falls quite heavily towards one shoulder, pulling him off line. If you notice that he always drifts in one direction, you can correct this in the short term with your rein contact, in the knowledge that as your training gradually straightens his body this issue will ultimately disappear. If, for example, he always drifts towards the right, you know that he is leaning on his right shoulder. In this case, always enter from the right rein (so that you have his right shoulder under control during the turn), and ride down the centre line with your right hand firmly pressed in against his withers, with a firmer contact on your right rein than your left. In the short term you may even need the right rein slightly shorter than the left one, or in very extreme cases you might need to take your right hand slightly across his withers, although this should only be considered as a very short-term correction as it points up a serious defect in his training.

'Came above bit on centre line'

You must get your horse's outline as round as you can in the minute or so that you have to ride around the arena before your test begins. If at all possible ride small circles to help you; by virtue of the geometry of a small circle his inside hind leg is placed further forward beneath his body than when on a straight line and, as long as you ride him actively forward into your contact, this extra engagement makes it easier to develop a round outline.

Placing of the hind legs on a 10 m circle. When a horse is correctly aligned to the small circle, his inside hind leg is further forward beneath his body than it is on a straight line.

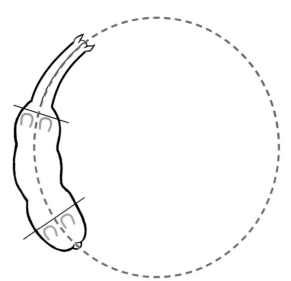

If you do not have the space to ride small circles, then use each corner to help: every corner is a quarter of a circle. Also, if you are able, use shoulder-fore or shoulder-in, or even just ask him to flex to one side whilst on the straight lines and ride him purposefully forward into your contact to round him up. Do not swing him rapidly from one flexion to the other; this does nothing other than wag his nose from side to side. Maintain flexion to the one side until you have him round, no matter how many strides this takes, and before changing to the other flexion and repeating.

Use your turn into the arena in the same way, so that you have the roundest outline possible when you begin your centre line, and it is then up to you to keep riding him positively forward into a secure contact to maintain it.

'Overbending on centre line'

Make sure that your horse is in as good an outline as you can achieve before you begin your turn into the arena. If he tries to duck his head downward, make some upward half-halts (a quick forward/upward flick of the contact designed to dislodge the bit from where he can lean onto it) combined with a stronger (but not quicker) leg aid to persuade him to step up into your contact. Try not to make any of your aiding too obvious! Repeat as necessary whilst on the centre line – this sort of issue often only happens inside the arena and you may have to sacrifice a few tests to get your message across, building obedience for the future.

'Deep and bearing down on centre line and getting faster'

Start your entry at a slow speed; once a horse has either his head down or he has gained too much speed, correction of these issues will be very hard. Again, make sure that he is in the best outline you can achieve before you enter the arena (this seems obvious, but with so many other things to think about it may not be foremost in your mind).

Practise riding centre lines at home and make him halt as soon as he tries to become deep or run forward. He will begin to anticipate this reaction from you and when he does, you can start to ride a half-halt instead of a full halt. This will rebalance him back onto his haunches, lifting his forehand and head and controlling his speed. Ultimately you can expect the same reaction from him in competition.

'Hurried down the centre line'

Possible culprits here are: over-riding, trying too hard, rider nerves, horse anticipation/anxiety, and loss of balance putting the horse on his forehand.

Plenty of good test experiences for both partners may help you both to become more relaxed, but you can also try the exercise described above under: 'Deep and bearing down on centre line and getting faster', employing frequent halts on the centre line in training until he listens enough for you to use just a half-halt to regulate both his speed and his balance.

'Above the bit/inattentive in halt'

If this happens habitually, not just as a one-off, you need to ride your horse into halt in a deeper outline than you would normally like, so that you have him really secure in your contact and in a position where you can feel him start to lift his head and prevent him from doing so before he has raised his head more than a little. Losing one mark for being 'slightly deep in halt' is better than losing two or three for being above the bit and lacking attention.

Also, if this is the halt at the start of your test it is even more important to keep him on your aids, or else your move-off, and potentially your first movement, may also be affected.

'Deep into/in halt'

Coming into halt in this manner is usually a method for a horse to evade taking the weight onto his hind legs; he is stopping himself by using a combination of his front legs and your hands for support.

You need to employ more half-halts as you approach your halt to encourage him to start taking more weight back onto his haunches, and then use the little 'upward' half-halts described above in 'Overbending on centre line' during the process of halting, to prevent him from leaning on your hands.

You should also check that there is no physical reason for him to be doing this (back problems or low-grade lameness, for example) and spend more time in training, teaching him to respond correctly to your half-halts and developing in him a genuine physical ability to take more weight behind as well as becoming more obedient to your aids.

'Crooked halt'

You have a choice here, depending on: 1) the degree of crookedness, and 2) your goal for that test.

A mildly crooked halt is almost always better left alone, especially at the earlier levels of competition, as attempting to correct it may cause a horse to become confused and anxious, potentially ending up with a worse halt than you started with! Bearing in mind that one of the major ingredients of the halt is *immobility*, it is better to keep him standing still than to teach him that it is acceptable to move *after* you have achieved a stationary position.

A very crooked halt should be corrected by riding forward a step or two, *not* by trying to push his quarters over behind you. Trying to move just the quarters will often result in fishtailing, when he will swing his haunches from side to side, almost certainly upsetting his balance and possibly making him move his shoulders to the side to regain stability. The result will be an even *more* crooked halt. Stepping forward will allow him to straighten and remain balanced. Obviously it will not gain you as high a mark as a straight halt at the first attempt, but is far more acceptable to the judge, and also better training in the long term.

If you are riding the test for training purposes you will be more likely to correct the straightness of a halt than if you are trying to win, when you might gain a better mark by leaving it alone.

If he habitually halts with his haunches to the same side, you are probably dealing with his natural crookedness (which you will be working on in his regular training), and until he is physically straighter try riding into halt with your leg further back on the side that he swings towards, and possibly more strongly pressed against his belly than your other leg. Even better, if you have a reasonable degree of control of his shoulders you could try putting him into a slight shoulder-fore position (towards the side to which he swings his haunches) just before and also during the halting process, to keep his shoulders in front of his haunches as he tries to move them to the side.

'Abrupt halt', 'anticipating halt'

Once they have done a few tests, many horses start to anticipate halting on the centre line and will often 'put the brakes on', either abruptly or before you reach the required marker. If you know that this is likely to happen:

- Avoid riding centre line halts in practice.

- In competition, ride really positively down the centre line and keep plenty of leg on your horse as you start to ask for the halt – it is most likely that you will not need to use any rein aids at all.

- Contrary to just about all other advice given, leave preparation for this halt until the very last moment!

'Fidgeting/stepping back in halt'

Possibilities to consider and adjust for the next test might be:

- Did you have too strong a rein contact into your halt? Next time try less or even no extra weight in your reins during the approach to the halt.

- Did you have your legs sufficiently on your horse to ride forward into your halt? If you used insufficient leg he may have left his hind legs trailing behind himself and as a consequence lacked stability in halt: next time *use* your legs during the transition.

- Did you relax your contact once you achieved your halt? Maintaining too strong a contact can make a horse feel trapped and uncomfortable. He may also think that you want rein-back and so once he achieves halt, slacken the reins slightly.

- Did you try to straighten a crooked halt after he stopped? Unless it was horribly crooked it is usually best to leave well alone once you have achieved immobility.

- Did you/do you habitually try to square him up? If you try this at too early a stage in his education, before he fully understands to move each hind leg individually in response to each of your legs, he is more likely to learn that you want him to move around rather than to be immobile in halt.

- Did you sit up and keep your weight fully in the saddle when you halted, or did you tip forward? (See the correct way to salute on pages 107–8.) Any shifting of your weight might cause him to move, and as lightening the weight in your seat is a component aid for rein-back, he might have made an assumption that this is what you were requesting. Try always to keep your full weight in the saddle both in your approach to the halt, and during it.

- Is he a naturally fidgety horse? Some horses do find it a trial to stand still, and you will need to keep your aids (legs, seat and rein) constantly slightly on during a halt to hold him still: not strongly enough that he feels trapped, but sufficient that you can keep him connected between your leg and hand and so fully attentive to you. You should also spend lots of time practising immobile halts at home and during the warm-up.

'Slow to move forward from halt'

Review your aiding (see page 109).

Was your halt sufficiently engaged? If your horse's hind legs trail in halt, there can be no possibility of a crisp move off, so this may be an area to address.

If he is just lazy to your aids, tackle this first in training:

1. Establish as good a halt as you can.

2. Ask him to move off directly into trot.

3. If he fails to respond crisply, immediately apply much stronger aids. This can involve both strong leg aids and your whip, and you must experiment until you get the response you want. Initially do not worry if he loses his outline or even canters instead of trotting: a forward response is all that should interest you and you must praise him when he gives it, no matter how messy. On the other hand, do not be satisfied with a transition that dribbles through walk.

4. Repeat, using a normal aiding level, and give him the opportunity to respond; if he does not respond instantly then do not hesitate to emphasise the aids again.

5. After a few repetitions, he should start to get the message and you can begin to take care of his outline and the quality of the trot that you achieve.

Always ride a halt and move-off during your competition warm-up: you may find that you need to repeat this sharpening-up procedure before you go to the arena to ride your test.

'Above the bit in move-off'

■ Did you throw the rein contact away as you asked your horse to move off? He needs a contact that is allowing, but definitely there.

■ You may need to do more training at home on his acceptance of the contact, and prior to moving off use a little vibration on both reins to ask him to stay softly yielding in his jaw and poll as he goes to trot.

■ It is also possible that he is not yet strong enough in his back to use it to lift his shoulders into the trot, and that he throws his head upward instead to lift his forehand, just as he would do when not under saddle. The solution to this is to do both strengthening work – schooling, hill work and pole work, all in a round frame – and to teach him *how* to use his back instead of defaulting to an uneducated way of using his body.

'Wobbled in move-off'; 'falling off centre line'

If you receive either of these comments it is likely that either your horse lacked sufficient impulsion in his move-off to support his balance, or that the halt you are moving out of was not straight. If the former is the problem, review 'Slow to move forward from halt' above, and focus on a more positive move-off coupled with keeping your eyes glued to the C marker.

If your initial halt was not totally straight and, as already advised, you chose not to correct it to preserve immobility, then you are starting from a position where he has more weight over one front leg than the other. You should be able to feel this: you might feel that you or he or indeed both of you are leaning towards that side, and/or that you have more weight in one rein than the other. When he moves off he is automatically going to step towards that side, as that is where his body-weight is pointing.

Again, your answer is to keep your eyes fixed on C and to ride forward with energy. With the hand that is carrying more weight (on the side towards which he is leaning), you should also close your fist tightly in against his withers until you can feel his skin against your knuckles. Also keep your elbow on this side closed tightly against your own ribcage. This closed rein prevents him from falling even further towards that shoulder as he moves forward, and with plenty of impulsion he will be straight on the centre line within a few steps.

'Drifted right/left before turn at C'

Review the aiding for this turn (see pages 103–4). If your horse drifted to the outside of the turn, one of the components of your aiding was either missing or insufficient; probably your weight distribution or your outside rein.

If he fell inward, you either had too much weight to the inside, or you needed to use a stronger inside leg aid to keep him upright and stepping sufficiently forward beneath himself to keep his balance.

It is also possible that he may have been backing off (spooking at) the judge's box/car, in which case you needed to keep his attention more definitely on you, using small vibrations along your inside rein to both demand attention and to flex him slightly towards the direction in which you are turning.

10 20 m Circles

You and your horse will perform more 20 m circles than any other movement throughout your careers, so paying attention to accurate riding of this figure early on makes sense. Even if you think that you know how, reviewing your precision is never wasted time; you may be surprised to find how easily your horse can take over and produce the shape *he* wants (not round, drifting away from the markers etc.) to evade the correct alignment of his body and therefore the engaging effects of the figure. If your attention is on other factors, such as keeping his outline round or maintaining his impulsion, he may be able to sneak such evasions in without you noticing.

WHAT THE JUDGE WANTS TO SEE

- That the quality and rhythm of your horse's gait shows no change before, during or after the circle.

- That there are no changes in his balance, outline or impulsion before, during or after the circle.

- That he has and maintains a continuous bend throughout his body length that matches the arc of the circle, with his footfalls showing correct tracking in alignment to the circle.

- A truly round circle that is correctly positioned so that it touches the required markers.

- A smooth entry and exit to the figure and to the bend at the start and the straightening at the end.

20 m Circles at A or C in the Short Arena

Example
'CXC circle left (20 m diameter).'

These are the easiest 20 m circles in many ways, as you have the most reference points to check: touching the track at C (or A), then at a halfway point between the corner and E (or B), touching X, then again halfway between B (or E) and the next corner.

It is relatively easy to estimate X, it being exactly in the centre of the school, but note that the *quarter markers* are of little use to you as reference points: they are 6 m from the corners, so neither at the place you must touch the track (i.e. at 10 m from the corner), nor even halfway to that point. (See also page 83.)

Initially, try thinking of your circle like a diamond: four points that you must touch, but where you must not allow your horse to linger.

Riding a 20 m circle in a short arena: the diamond shape indicates the four touch points.

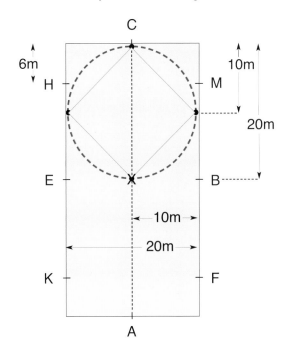

One of the most common faults with 20 m circles is when the horse clings to the track, travelling along it for three or more strides until the circle develops straight sections and begins to be more like a square. Learn to **touch the track for just one stride**, and then leave it again, heading directly to your next touch point. Once you have this degree of control, start to allow the lines between your touch points to become curved instead of straight, but continue to exercise this precision of riding with just the one stride on the track.

Become aware of where you are heading as you pass over X. Very often circles develop a 'bulge' towards the track after crossing the centre line. Make it a habit that as you pass over X, *you are already pointing* towards your next touch point.

Another common error is to ride around the short side as if you were going large: this will give you a circle with two corners, i.e. an incorrect shape.

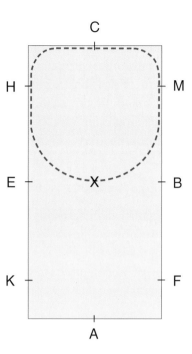

20 m circle with corners through the short side.

Admittedly in the earlier stages of training you will ride the short sides more like a half 20 m circle, but to produce a correctly shaped circle you must *lose the habit* of simply following the track, especially if you compete in an arena that has developed a marked track with a clear short side with corners! Make sure that you pay attention to your touch points and ride as if the track does not exist.

20 m Circles at A and C in the Long Arena

Again, you need to be aware of the misleading position – in terms of relevance to your circle – of the extra markers found in the long arena: R, S, V and P. These markers are 18 m from the corner, and so you must ride a couple of metres *beyond* the line that intersects them with the centre line. (See the diagram on page 84.)

20 m Circles at Other Markers

You can also ride 20 m circles at V, E, S, R, B and P, (or anywhere that you choose in a freestyle test). Your best guide to accuracy here is to practise developing a feel for the size of the circle in terms of how much you need to turn your body (muscle memory) and how much bend you need in your horse. Also pay strict attention to the two reference points that you *do* have: S and R, E and B, V and P. Ensure that you touch the track at the opposite point (for one stride only) to your starting point, and that you clearly finish the circle at exactly the place where it began.

PREPARATION

About two strides before you reach the marker, lightly vibrate your inside rein to begin asking for inside flexion and start to turn your upper body to the inside. This will give your horse sufficient warning so that when you arrive at the marker and give a squeeze with your inside lower leg, he is ready to contract his inside ribcage muscles to produce the required bend, and is prepared mentally to move his shoulders away from the psychological support of the track.

Starting the Circle

1. As your horse's nose arrives at the marker, turn your upper body sufficiently for the degree of bend appropriate to a 20 m circle (practise getting this feel at home).

2. Allow your weight to drop slightly into your inside seat bone and stirrup, taking care *not* to lean your upper body over. This is achieved by moving your outside leg slightly back into an outside leg position, where it will rest lightly against his side to discourage/prevent his quarters from swinging out.

3. In response to these aids, his shoulders will start to leave the track as your body comes level with the marker.

(*Left*) Correct outside leg position, with the whole leg drawn back from the hip. (*Right*) Commonly seen position of the outside leg: here it has no ability to control the haunches.

Maintaining the Circle

If you have begun correctly, and you are keeping a check on any reference points available, your main focus for the remainder of the 20 m circle should be on maintaining the rhythm and quality of your horse's gait. You must also monitor the consistency of his bend, outline and balance, and make any adjustments necessary, but if your preparation in training and in setting up the movement has been sufficient, these will pretty much take care of themselves.

Finishing the Circle

As the horse's nose comes back to the track *at the marker*, begin to straighten your shoulders until you are looking straight along the track in front of you and equalise the weight in your two seat bones. Stay relaxed in your arms with a forward-feeling contact.

TROUBLESHOOTING

'Circle too large'; 'drifting out'; 'poor shape'

Whilst accuracy must always be a secondary consideration to the quality of a horse's way of going (relaxation, rhythm and suppleness are your primary concerns at this level), drifting outward or deliberately making the figure too large or misshapen (regardless of whose choice it is – his or yours) will be seen by the judge as an avoidance of the purpose of the exercise. The purpose of all circles is to produce a degree of engagement of a horse's inside hind leg, courtesy of the geometry of the figure which brings his inside hind leg further forward beneath his body (see diagram on page 111).

To correct these issues, first check your body position and weight distribution.

■ Are you turning your upper body sufficiently (outside shoulder forward/inside shoulder back)?

■ Are your elbows staying at your sides? If they lift upward or move forward, you will lose the integrity of your outside rein contact, allowing your horse room to escape through the gap that you have created.

■ Is your weight clearly in your inside seat bone and stirrup? If your seat (and/or saddle) has slipped or been pushed to the outside, your weight may be pulling him outward.

If these requirements are all in place, correct your horse by:

■ Closing your outside rein contact more firmly against his neck to control his outside shoulder. As your shoulders turn, your outside hand must have a feeling of *pushing* towards his inside ear, but with your upper arm and elbow snug against your ribcage. *Press* the rein more firmly against the outside of his neck, almost as though you are neck reining, but *never* take your hand across to the other side of his neck/withers because, while this would successfully turn his shoulders, it would also ask for the opposite bend. You might feel your knuckles pressing into his crest – this is fine.

■ Opening your inside hand away from his neck. Still keep your elbow at your side and move just your forearm to the inside in a leading/ opening rein effect.

Outside rein closed tightly against the neck.

■ Increase the amount of weight in your inside stirrup and seat bone. His body will involuntarily move inward to stay beneath your weight and you must then use more inside leg to send him actively forward as his body-weight arrives above his inside hind leg.

■ In certain cases you may need to use your outside leg to help control the outside of his body; make sure that it is moved back *from the hip* into an outside leg position (see photograph on page 121). Moving just the lower leg back does not have the correct effect on your seat, i.e. that your hips parallel his hips and that your outside seat bone is slightly lifted up inside your buttock muscle, redistributing the weight of your seat towards your inside seat bone. You may need to use just the lower leg, or you may need to close the whole leg against his side to get the effect you require, which is that he neither swings his quarters out, nor drifts outward on his circle.

'Falling in'; 'falling onto inside shoulder'; 'circle too small'; 'wrong bend'; 'lacking bend'; 'lacking suppleness'

Whilst these are not necessarily all the same problem, the solution in a test situation is the same: you need to move your horse's shoulders/body towards the outside of your circle and increase the bend throughout the length of his body.

Start by checking that you are not the cause.

■ If you are leaning to the inside, or have too much weight in your inside seat bone, you may be pulling him over/inward.

■ Did you use sufficient inside leg to ask for the bend?

■ Did you ask for sufficient impulsion? Without this the circle size may deteriorate.

■ Are you *allowing* enough with your outside rein to permit him to bend to the inside? This should be as a result of correct upper-body positioning (i.e. outside shoulder forward), and a forward-feeling contact.

If the above points are not issues, correct your horse by:

■ Equalising the weight in your two seat bones.

■ Using an *indirect* rein by moving your inside hand inwards towards his shoulder, or even across his withers to press his shoulders to the outside and ensure they are upright. This will also bend his neck to the inside; make sure that your *outside* rein is not so strong that you make this impossible for him, or cause him to stiffen his neck. (**Remember**, this is a short-term fix for the duration of a test and should not be used in training.)

■ Use your inside leg, starting with just your lower leg, to ask him to contract his inside ribcage muscles to produce body bend. If he bends, he can't lean.

■ If the lower leg alone is not sufficient, use your upper leg as well with a feeling of pushing his whole middle section towards the outside.

■ Have a feeling of continually leg-yielding towards the outside of your circle. This will both prevent him from falling/leaning in, and create a better connection from your inside leg to your outside hand.

On the home training front you need to work to develop more suppleness throughout the length of his body using exercises including smaller circles (e.g. 15 m), trotting poles on a curve, and leg-yielding done in a training fashion (i.e. encouraging him to bend his whole body to the inside whilst he steps sideways). Physiotherapy exercises such as carrot stretches can also be highly beneficial.

'Losing quarters to the outside'

If this problem is not just a result of less-than-careful riding (i.e. not using a correct outside leg position – see photograph on page 121), this might indicate:

■ Stiffness or lack of use of the lateral bending (ribcage) muscles.

■ Stiffness of the hind leg joints leading to unwillingness to bend them sufficiently to step the inside hind leg forward beneath the body.

■ Laziness, producing a deliberate avoidance of the correct alignment and so avoiding the extra effort needed to engage his inside hind beneath his body.

If you watch closely (maybe have a video made) you will see that his inside hind leg travels with straight joints, swinging forward from the hip joint alone with no bend in stifle, hock or fetlock joints, and crosses over in front of his outside hind.

To correct the problem:

■ You must develop a true bend throughout his length as a result either of improving his suppleness or his obedience to your leg aids. This is largely a training issue, although in competition it may mean simply that you must be more conscientious about the correct position and use of your inside and outside legs on the circle.

■ Other training exercises such as raised trotting poles can help, and physiotherapy can also be useful here.

■ If it is a deliberate evasion, again be extremely strict with yourself about correct leg positions, using a stronger outside leg to hold your horse's haunches in place with a feeling of *almost* riding haunches-in, and then use a more insistent inside leg to demand that he steps actively forward with his inside hind.

'Falling out; 'leaning on the outside shoulder'; 'too much neck bend'; 'travelling with haunches in'

At first glance these errors might not seem connected, but they are in reality all aspects of the same problem: the horse who is losing balance towards his outside shoulder.

In the competition arena this is readily corrected by taking more outside rein to stop his shoulder from falling outward. It might mean that you have a lot of weight in your outside hand for the duration of the circle, but then it is up to you

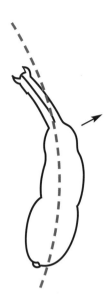

Falling/leaning onto the outside shoulder: this is most often seen with an excessive inside neck bend and sometimes with the haunches also displaced slightly to the inside.

to do more work at home in between shows to improve his straightness. For a short-term solution at the show, simply close your outside elbow tightly against your side and push your outside hand right in against his withers with the outside rein pressed against his neck (see photograph on page 123).

Do not try to correct this by attempting to push his haunches outward – this will result in a loss of engagement. **Always** correct straight-ness issues by re-placing his forehand in front of his haunches, not the other way around.

'Leaning in on circle'

You can achieve surprisingly small circles with a horse who leans in. It is not, however, correct because leaning and bending are mutually exclusive and so leaning is an avoidance of bend.

Initially, leaning may be the result of a lack of suppleness or a lack of understand-

Leaning in on the circle: Bertie has too much bend in his neck whilst his body lacks bend altogether: to achieve the circle he is leaning to the inside. Mary has tried to position her outside leg correctly for the circle but has leaned to the inside at the same angle as Bertie.

ing of the aids, but it may also be an avoidance of engagement as described above under 'losing quarters to the outside'.

Pay attention to how upright you feel *relative to the ground*, **not** to your horse.

Correcting the problem of leaning involves better preparation for the circle so that the horse is in his best possible engagement and balance before you begin the figure. You must also, I repeat, pay close attention to *your own position*, staying upright relative to the ground *not* to your horse, and producing the correct body position and aids for the circle. As a rider it is all too easy to lean inward and your horse will certainly turn onto and produce a circle but just not in the way we want to see it done!

For persistent leaning you may need to exaggerate some corrective aids.

■ Keep your weight equal in both seat bones rather than weighting the inside one.

■ In the short-term it may possibly help to even take your weight towards the *outside* of the saddle to bring his body upright.

■ Use your whole inside leg – upper leg, lower leg and your knee – to push his ribcage up and outward.

None of these corrective aids should be used long term. This is a serious training issue that needs dealing with before you progress beyond the most basic levels or else it will hamper the development of his balance, suppleness and engagement.

11 Two 20 m Circles/Half-circles

These movements can also be described as a figure-of-eight, although they are not referred to as such on test sheets.

Example 1
'B turn right, X circle right 20 m diameter; X circle left 20 m diameter; E turn left.'

Example 2
'A half-circle right 20 m diameter; X circle left 20 m diameter; X half-circle right 20 m diameter.'

Two 20 m circles meeting through X.

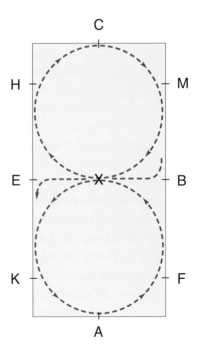

WHAT THE JUDGE WANTS TO SEE

- A good quality working trot with the same rhythm, tempo and activity maintained throughout the figure.

- A consistent outline with no resistance or stiffening through the change of bend over X.

- Supple bending with correct and equal alignment to both circles and no leaning to the inside (horse or rider!).

And for Example 1

- A smooth turn at B that is clearly a turn rather than one quarter of a 20 m circle yet is not so sharp as to cause loss of balance, straightness or rhythm. Note the difference of the track in the diagram.

- A short, straight line after the turn so that you arrive at X, directly facing E.

- A true, round 20 m circle that clearly starts at X and returns to X.

- A straight horse as you pass over X, facing *directly towards* E for one stride during the change of direction.

- A second 20 m circle with the same criteria as above.

- Upon returning to X a straight line heading directly towards E followed by a smooth turn onto the track that is clearly a turn and not a continuation of the previous circle.

And for Example 2

- A clear difference between the line you ride as you pass through the corner preceding A and the beginning of your first circle, where you should not ride into the corner.

- That your horse is straight as you pass over X, facing directly towards (in this case) the B marker for one stride during each change of direction.

- That after you finish the second half circle at A, you then ride *into* the following corner.

To summarise the main points:

- Show clear differences between your turns and your circle lines.

- Always pass through X with a straight horse, totally aligned on the half school (E-B) line.

PRESENTATION

Riding the Change of Direction Through X

1. During the half of the 20 m circle preceding X your horse will be in a clear bend from nose to tail that matches the arc of the circle, with (in both examples) your upper body turned to the right.

2. During the last few strides *before* reaching X, straighten your shoulders and start to press your *left* lower leg against his ribcage to begin losing the right bend.

3. If you are in rising trot, change your diagonal, preferably a stride *before* X, but certainly not later than X as he needs time to react to the change of direction and this warns him that it is coming.

4. As he passes over X, turn your shoulders to the left and keep pressing with your left leg so that he begins to produce left bend.

5. Also in this stride, slightly increase the weight in your left seat bone/stirrup (without leaning your upper body to the side). This slight displacement of your combined centre of gravity will start the left hand circle as you leave X.

TROUBLESHOOTING

Most of the problems associated with producing these figures in competition result from inaccurate riding and can be solved by going back over the instructions given above.

Change of bend issues need to be worked on in training so that his understanding of the response you require to your leg aids for bending, i.e. contraction of his ribcage muscles, is clearer, and that his body becomes more supple so that he can manage both bends with greater ease and equality.

Loss of balance/changes of speed during the change of direction will be due either to lack of suppleness – for which more work at home is required – or to you rushing through the change of direction, the worst being if you *lean over to the side*. Throwing your weight suddenly from one side to the other will certainly cause him to change direction, but will also pull him off balance causing him to change speed and/or to stiffen. Be very conscientious about sitting up straight and turning your upper body from one side to the other without leaning over – the weight changes in your stirrup/seat bone should be subtle – and take *time* about it: don't hurry your aiding.

12 15 m, 12 m, and 10 m Circles

WHAT THE JUDGE WANTS TO SEE

All the features required for 20 m circles are required for the following smaller-sized circles.

15 m Circles

To ride accurate 15 m circles takes judgement and a fair degree of spatial awareness (see Chapter 8 for guidance on improving your spatial awareness). Circles that start from the markers on the long sides require you to estimate the location of the opposite quarter line (sometimes also called the three-quarter line), as the position of the apex of your circle, whilst circles ridden at A, C, or X need you to estimate 2½ m from the track on either side.

Put simply, the quarter line is located halfway between the centre line and the track. Picture in your mind the centre line drawn onto the ground, and then estimate a halfway point between your imaginary line and the edge of the arena.

Practice will ensure you discover how much you need to turn your shoulders to create the appropriate bend for this size of circle. You should aim to touch the quarter line for just one stride before continuing on around the second half of your circle with the goal of returning to the track at exactly the marker where you originally left it.

Riding 15 m circles at A and C takes even more judgement: at one quarter and three quarters of the way around your circle you must be 2½ m from the track (see diagram on following page). Try striding this out on your feet, or even measuring it, and put a marker to one side or the other of the exact distance (such as in the photograph on page 85 where cones have been used to mark out a 10 m circle) so that you can ride either around it or just inside it to get used to how this size of circle should feel.

For a 15 m circle at X, you must be the same distance away from the sides of the arena as above, and also 5 m away from either A or C.

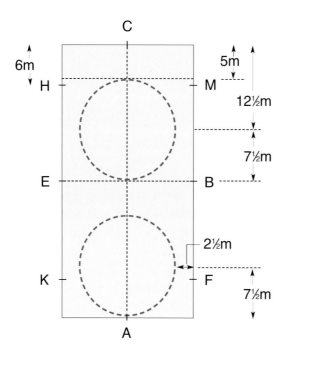

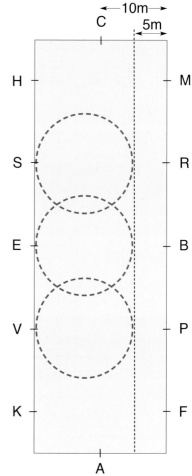

Positions for riding 15 m circles. (*Left*) Circles ridden at A and X. (*Right*) Circles ridden on the long side showing the quarter line (dotted line).

12 m Circles

These are less easy to judge: the best way to estimate a 12 m circle is to become proficient at riding 10 m circles, and then simply ride the 12 m circle a little bigger than the 10 m ones!

10 m Circles

A circle of 10 m diameter or less is also known as a *volte*.

Judging the size of a 10 m circle is relatively simple when it is required at any marker on the long side: start accurately at the marker, touch the centre line, and return precisely to the same marker. It sounds simple, doesn't it? But unless your horse is sufficiently prepared, both at home (suppleness) and in the test (giving him sufficient warning before you arrive at the marker), all sorts of problems can occur. These include:

- Circle too large.

- Egg-shaped circles.

- Arriving back at the track at a completely different place to your point of departure.

- Loss of balance onto the forehand.

- Loss of balance to the outside shoulder (drifting out).

- Horse (and sometimes rider also) leaning inward, bicycle-style (see photograph on page 126).

- Quarters swinging out.

- Loss of impulsion (slowing down).

Positions for riding 10 m circles on the long side and at A (or C), with the quarter lines shown (dotted lines).

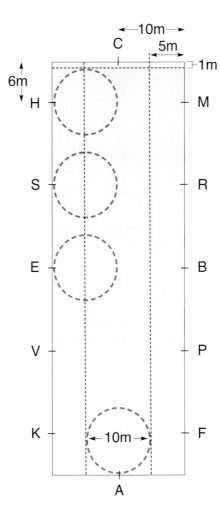

- Loss of rhythm.

- Loss of suspension/cadence (spring in his steps).

Judging the size at either A or C requires you to estimate the figure more by feel than by reference points. These circles will touch the quarter lines on both sides, but probably the best way to ride such circles is by practising plenty of 10 m circles at home and memorising how they *feel*, in terms of how much you need to turn your body and how much bend you need in your horse. As always, practice at home, possibly with visible markers (e.g. cones) to guide you, makes perfect.

PREPARATION

Preparation should be the same as for 20 m circles.

Starting the Circles

As for 20 m circles, you must adjust the amount of upper-body turn according to the arc of whichever sized circle you are going to ride. Practice, practice!

Maintaining 15 m Circles

Maintenance of the 15 m circle is as for 20 m circles. Although the arc of this circle is tighter, it is still a fairly large circle and once you have the feel for it, it should cause you no more difficulties than riding the 20 m circle.

Maintaining 12 m and 10 m Circles

As long as your preparation was fine and you started your circle correctly, your main focus should now be on impulsion. Due to the tighter arc of these smaller circles your horse must step further forward with his inside hind leg beneath his body, which means that he must make a greater effort. Once you are competent at riding each size and shape accurately, try to think of each circle as being in two halves.

1. The first half is your set-up, when you establish his balance and a relaxed, soft bend.

2. In the second half these factors should take care of themselves, and you can now ask for a stronger trot (or canter) using stronger (but not quicker) leg aids. Make sure that your hands have a forward *pushing* feel, not a tight, over-controlling feel.

Your goal is to finish each circle with *more* impulsion than you started with, or at the very least the same, but never with less.

Finishing Smaller Circles

Finishing these smaller circles is the same as for 20 m circles. In the case of the 12 m and 10 m circles, if you have ridden them as described you should find that you are moving along the track with increased impulsion.

TROUBLESHOOTING

'Circle too large'; 'falling out'; 'poor shape'

With these faults the possibilities are:

■ You did not prepare adequately in terms of how he was moving during your approach. He was probably out of balance as a result of travelling too fast, or of being on his forehand. Next time pay more attention to his balance during the steps preceding the circle, making half-halts as needed.

■ You failed to warn him of the approaching circle and as a consequence he took too long to react when you began the figure.

■ Your work at home has not yet adequately suppled his body for the demands of these figures.

■ You didn't turn your upper body sufficiently for the arc of the circle, or you held your outside rein too tightly to allow him to bend his body into alignment with the figure.

■ You allowed your outside arm/elbow to lift away from your ribcage, or your outside arm straightened so that your fist moved forward independently of your body. All of these give him the freedom to drift out through his outside shoulder. Next time make sure that you keep your elbow bent, in and down whilst still having the feeling of pushing the contact forward.

■ You rode with a lack of accuracy, not taking enough care over noticing your start/finish points, or over the degree to which you were turning your upper body.

■ Your weight slipped or was pushed to the outside, pulling him off balance so that he had to move outward to stay beneath you. Make a deliberate effort to move your hips (and probably also your saddle) to the inside, with increased weight in your inside stirrup and a stronger outside leg aid to demand that he lifts his outside back muscle up underneath the saddle.

- He was deliberately making the circle too large to avoid the engaging effect and so the greater effort demanded by the accurately sized/shaped figure. Become aware of this evasion and use more outside rein pressure against his neck combined with more weight in your inside seat bone/stirrup and stronger outside leg aids to control the outside of his body.

'Too much neck bend'; 'needs more bend through the body'

If he is genuinely capable of the bend required, then you probably tried to turn onto the circle by pulling the inside rein. Next time take more care with your preparation and body positioning and try to *push* him around with your *outside* rein rather than pulling on the inside one which will result in too much neck bend, too little body bend and loss of impulsion.

'Falling inward'; 'leaning in'; 'circle too small'; 'almost wrong bend'

He either lacked sufficient bend in his body (lack of suppleness, or your outside rein was too tight to allow the bend), or you had too much weight to the inside thus pulling him off balance. The horse who is leaning onto his inside shoulder may well be looking slightly to the outside, and the circle will become progressively smaller. Leaning and bending are mutually exclusive, so the horse who is leaning over bicycle-style is not contracting his inside ribcage muscles (intercostals), so avoiding drawing his inside hind leg forward beneath his body, i.e. engaging.

First check that your weight distribution and/or outside rein contact are not causes. If they are not, then you need to work on more suppleness in his training, with bend being a direct result of contracting his intercostal muscles in response to the stimulus of your inside leg in the girth position – always assuming that you *used* your inside leg in the first place!

Having done more suppling work at home, when you next compete make sure that your aiding of the bend is clear, with correct body positioning from you and rhythmic squeezes of your inside leg at the girth to demand that he bends through his entire length from nose to tail.

If, despite all these preparations, he still falls inward, use the corrections described under the same heading, but for 20 m circles (see page 124).

Falling in on the circle may also be a result of lack of impulsion (see below).

'Losing impulsion on circle'; 'losing (or lacking) suspension/cadence'

If you had everything correctly organised for your circle, he will need to make a greater effort to maintain his impulsion than he will on a straight line or a circle of larger diameter. Many horses need to be prompted to make this effort.

Be aware of his *tempo* (the speed of his footfalls). If you notice this slowing down, then he is losing impulsion. Make a deliberate effort to use your rhythmic leg aids (and your rising, if you are in rising trot) at a constant speed, *not* following *his* speed. Horses take the speed of their rhythm from the speed of your aiding, so insist that he keeps up to *your* speed.

You can also use a stronger squeeze to ask for a stronger step, but do *not* aid out of rhythm.

If necessary back up your leg with a tap from your schooling whip.

'Losing rhythm'

Loss of rhythm on a small circle may have several different possible causes:

- Loss of impulsion. As he slows down and becomes laboured, the natural differences between his two sides become more obvious, and he may push more strongly off one hind leg than the other, causing an unequal rhythm.

- Lack of suppleness. A stiff horse will be unable to move fluently around the small arc of the circle, although he will probably by markedly better in one direction than in the other. You need to address this in training.

- Loss of balance. This may be either onto the forehand, or laterally toward one or other shoulder, and can be improved with more care in the preparation before the circle.

- Lack of submission to the contact. If he stiffens his body either laterally or longitu- dinally, he will be unable to move fluently around the small circle. Problems with submission may be schooling issues, or momentary issues such as spooking or a lack of adequate preparation time to allow him to organise his body in such a way as to comply easily with your request.

'Losing quarters'; 'quarters swinging out'

Causes are:

- Lack of suppleness (training issue).
- Lack of rider's attention to correct alignment.

- An incorrect outside leg position.

- Loss/lack of balance.

- Deliberate evasion of engagement.

Careful, correct preparation may avoid this problem. In the case of deliberate evasion you need to be very conscientious about your *outside* leg, making sure that it is truly in an outside leg position (see the photograph on page 121), and using it to displace his haunches slightly inward, producing *almost* a feeling of haunches-in, then use more inside leg to motivate him to step energetically forward with greater engagement.

13 Transitions Down and Up

Trot/Walk/Trot Transitions

Example
'Between K and A transition to walk (2-5 steps) and proceed in working trot.'

The test sheet will specify a precise number of steps for the walk, e.g. 3-7 steps; 2-5 steps, etc. As already discussed: to count the number of walk steps, simply count each front footfall: right fore 1; left fore 2; right fore 3; left fore 4. This counts as four steps.

WHAT THE JUDGE WANTS TO SEE

- A well-prepared, not abrupt downward transition that shows some indication that your horse is taking a little more weight onto his haunches during the transition (see page 91 for more details about downward transitions).

- A clean change from a trot sequence to a walk sequence with no shuffling or jogging.

- The specified number of walk steps in a good, clear, relaxed four-beat walk with obvious energy.

- An enthusiastic and direct departure into trot.

- No change in his outline during the execution of any part of this movement.

Once again, the important features are the quality of the way the work is done, i.e. the transitions and the gaits, and not just the accuracy.

PREPARATION
As ever, this is your key to a successful performance. From training, you should know how far ahead you will need to start warning your horse of an impending

transition and apply the same time frame here. If the test sheet calls for this movement to happen between two markers, aim to make your downward transition within a step or two of passing the first letter, so begin your preparation as you approach the letter, not once you have arrived at it.

There are certain circumstances when you might leave it until further past the marker, and these will be discussed below in the Troubleshooting section.

PRESENTATION

1. Try to achieve your downward transition with as soft a contact as you can manage, using small vibrations along the reins if he offers any resistance in his jaw, and with your legs **on**. Many riders put their legs on *just after* the transition, and think that they have used them *during* the transition. Try instead to close both your lower legs slightly further back against his belly as you prepare, and then keep them on *throughout* the transition, asking for the change of gait by holding your seat and upper body still with a slight resistance in your contact.

2. Relax your aids immediately he breaks into walk, following the movement with your hips and slightly with your contact. Start to count his steps from his first clear walk step. If you need to motivate the walk use alternate legs (left-right-left-right) so that he understands to stay in walk and does not misinterpret your aids to change to the trot.

3. As soon as you have counted the minimum number of clear steps, close both your legs at the same time and introduce a feeling of springing forward/upward with your hips to ask for the trot. If your downward transition was correct he will have plenty of impulsion and be ready to spring immediately into a lively trot. Do not leave it until later: if he takes more than one stride to respond you may find that you have too many walk steps.

4. As soon as he trots, re-establish the same speed and rhythm as you had before the transitions.

Transitions Ridden 'Before' or 'Over' a Marker

Examples

- 'Before X transition to walk (2-5 steps) and proceed in working trot.'
- 'Over A: transition to walk (2-5 steps) and then working trot.'

WHAT THE JUDGE WANTS TO SEE

The judge will expect to see all the features described under 'What the Judge Wants to See' for Trot/Walk/Trot transitions, with the downward transition performed before the specified marker and the upward transition after it.

PREPARATION

Prepare as for any other downward transition, but in these examples you will need to use a little more judgement: your goal is to position the two transitions equidistant from the specified marker, showing a little more planning and knowledge of your horse's individual reactions. When asked for 2–5 steps of walk to be shown, you should aim to be in clear walk early enough that you can show 2 walk steps before your body comes level with the marker.

PRESENTATION

The first example is perhaps more self-explanatory: you should make the downward transition as instructed, just *before* the marker (X, in this example) aiming to be in clear walk a couple of steps before X. Proceed with the rest of the movement as described earlier in this chapter.

When asked to perform transitions 'over' a marker, try to place the centre of the movement (i.e. the walk steps) as you ride in front of the specified marker. In other words: 1) make your downward transition a few metres *before* A; 2) ride clear walk steps as you pass in front of A; 3) make your upward transition after you have *passed* A. **Do not** make your downward transition *at* the specified marker, in this case A.

Canter/Trot/Canter Transitions

Example
'C circle left 20 m and over X: canter/trot/canter transition.'

A set number of steps of trot is not specified with canter/trot/canter transitions but the directive is that you should trot for 'one to two horse lengths' (a horse is roughly two and a half metres long).

WHAT THE JUDGE WANTS TO SEE

- A smooth transition to trot several metres before X with no resistance or change of outline, with the horse taking more weight onto the hind legs.

- Rhythmic and unhurried steps of trot for around one to two horse lengths (say, between three to five metres) as you pass over X.

- A smooth and enthusiastic yet relaxed transition up to canter.

- A consistent bend and outline maintained throughout.

PREPARATION

- Pay attention to the shape and correct placement of your circle.

- Try to have him in the best possible canter that you can achieve, in terms of balance and outline, and make sure that he is listening to you.

PRESENTATION

1. Once you are about one quarter of the way around the circle, start making small half-halts on your inside rein (little, brief squeezes) to encourage him to collect (take weight back onto his haunches) in preparation for the transition.

2. Make the downward transition with a small half-halt on your outside rein. At the same time move your outside leg slightly forward (it should have been in a true outside leg position until now (see the photograph on page 121). Do not try to move both of your legs back as you should in a trot/walk transition, as this may cause confusion if you ride, or start trying to teach your horse, flying changes.

3. Swing your seat in a trot rhythm for two or three strides.

4. Initiate the upward transition to canter by sliding your outside leg back and closing it against his side, combined with a downward and forward push of your inside seat bone into the saddle. If your horse is also used to an inside leg aid, do this by deepening your inside leg position: push your calf forward and down against his side, **do not** tighten your calf muscle, which will raise your heel and lighten your inside seat bone. Make sure to keep sitting up tall and to *keep* your contact throughout the transition.

TROUBLESHOOTING

'Against the hand to walk'

- Did you give him enough warning prior to asking for the transition? If you left it too late and 'put the brakes on' with your hands, he has every right to protest.

- Did you ask for the transition correctly? If you used just your hands, then you gave him no chance to transfer weight to his haunches: he will have to raise his head and brace his forehand to take the momentum of his body-weight.

- Are your transitions good enough in training? If your combined techniques are poor, a test situation will only exacerbate their appearance.

'Needs to be more forward in transition to walk'

You either used too strong a hand aid, or insufficient leg; riding a forward transition into a lower gait is dependent on finding the appropriate balance between leg and hand aids for that individual horse. With the less forward horse you may not need to use any hand aid at all.

'Walk steps not clear'; 'hurried in walk'; 'jogging'; 'not enough walk steps'

The competition atmosphere can make either or both of you tense and this often makes walk a difficult gait to produce clearly: a pure walk sequence is only possible when the horse's long back muscles on either side of his spine are alternately relaxed.
The possibilities here are:

- You may not have truly completed the transition before you relaxed your aids, making it unclear to your horse that he was supposed to be walking.

- You may not have relaxed your legs/seat/contact sufficiently to give him the confidence to relax himself.

- He may be anticipating the upward transition.

- You may have begun counting steps before he was clearly in walk. Even if his downward transition takes time to complete, you must not start counting the steps until he is clearly in a walk sequence.

If this problem happens even in training, take the time after each downward transition to walk on a contact for quite a way, possibly as much as half of a long side, before asking him to return to trot. You need to establish the *habit* of walking in a clear sequence immediately after the transition.

'Late to trot'; 'lazy to trot'; 'inattentive to the aid'

Your horse may have momentarily taken his attention away from you, but if you rode your downward transition competently, he has no excuse for a slow response.

If this happens, be quick to use a sharper aid even in the test: you don't want him to learn that he can be unresponsive in a test situation or else he will soon start to ignore all your aids in the arena. Horses do learn quite quickly that riders are less prepared to take them to task in the competition arena and sometimes it is necessary to throw a test away for the sake of making a point.

When training, work to get a sharper response and, as discussed in the Troubleshooting section for the horse who is 'slow to move forward from halt' (page 115), re-cover this issue both in the warm-up arena and during your circuit of the competition arena before your entry.

'Tried to canter in upward transition to trot'

An upward transition to trot is often required whilst you are riding a curve: either in a corner or on a circle. Try to make it very clear to your horse that you mean trot, not canter, by sitting with equal weight in your two seat bones, and when you swing your pelvis upward and forward for the transition make sure you *keep* the weight and lift equal in both sides. One of the major differences between the aids for trot and for canter is the extra weight you should put into your inside seat bone for a canter depart.

If this still does not sort things out for him, then lose any bend you have in his body during the walk steps, (straighten him by taking more outside rein) even on a curve. It is only for a brief moment and the judge is looking more keenly at the clarity of his gaits and transitions than at small details such as the slight bend you would have on such a gradual curve. Reinstate the bend once you are safely back into trot.

If this movement is to be performed in a corner, make both transitions a little later, so that your upward transition happens on the straight line of the short side, after you have exited the corner but before you reach the A or the C marker.

'Against the hand to trot' (in a downward transition)

■ Did you warn your horse that you were going to ask for a downward transition or did you suddenly 'apply the brakes'?

■ Did you ask him for a small degree of collection as you approached the transition? This is his warning signal: small half-halts on the inside rein in the canter.

■ Are his transitions of good enough quality at home or do you need to work on them more in training?

■ The extra distractions of a show can mean that he is not paying you as much attention as he does in training, requiring a stronger aid to achieve the transition; *insist* that he pays attention to you.

'Above the bit to trot/canter' (in an upward transition)

Did you startle your horse or use too strong an aid? If your downward transition was good, he will be ready and waiting for the upward transition and you should need only the smallest of aids to achieve it.

If he has a habit of going above the bit in upward transitions, take the opportunity during the steps between transitions to put him into a slightly over-deep outline, then when he lifts his head he will only come up into position, not above it.

'Ran to canter'; 'tense canter transition'

Such errors in a test are usually down to small errors in aiding your horse:

■ Leaning forward, so overloading his shoulders.

■ Dropping the contact – allowing him to lose balance and/or to run.

■ Hurrying either the aids or the preceding steps.

Correct these errors and there should be no further problem unless he either lacks respect for your leg aids in general or he is anxious about the canter transition, both of which need attention in training.

14 Two 10 m Half-circles

This movement can be performed in walk, trot and canter; in canter it is performed with a simple change of legs in the centre and will be covered in Chapter 26.

Example

'A, medium walk; B, half-circle left 10 m to X; X, half-circle right 10 m to E; E working trot.'

Two 10 m half-circles showing straight section over X.

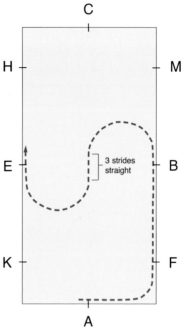

WHAT THE JUDGE WANTS TO SEE

- In walk: a good quality gait throughout the movement with active and enthusiastic but unhurried steps in a clear four-beat rhythm.

- In trot: rhythmic, elastic and enthusiastic steps throughout the movement with no loss of suspension (spring) or impulsion.

- A relaxed horse with a loose, swinging back.

- A consistently rounded outline with soft acceptance of the contact.

- An upright horse with clear spinal alignment to both half-circles, showing equally supple bend in both directions.

- Two smooth, well-shaped half-circles of equal size linked by a short, straight section over X, showing no loss of balance, resistance, stiffening or sudden jerky movements through the change of direction.

In Walk

PREPARATION

First, you need to have an active medium walk: think of it as a march, with a brisk but unhurried tempo. Have your reins at a comfortable length, i.e. shorter than a stretched (or free) walk, but not so short as to restrict him in either his neck or steps. If in doubt, err on the side of having longer reins in favour of freedom for the walk.

About two strides before B start to prepare him for the bend by making small vibrations on your left rein and by squeezing your left lower leg against his belly at the girth.

PRESENTATION

1. As the horse's nose comes to the marker, turn your shoulders to the left and put a *little* more weight into your left seat bone and stirrup.

2. Keep riding energetically **forward** so that he does not turn too sharply.

3. As your body comes level with B his shoulders should already have left the track, and his body be correctly bent for the arc of this quite small circle. His whole body should finish leaving the track as his tail passes the marker.

4. Ride your half-circle a little deeper than you would if you were going to ride a full circle at the marker; you are going to need to finish it a stride or two *before* X so that you have a few straight strides on the centre line before you begin your second half circle.

5. Look at X and imagine you are riding *a turn onto the centre line* and that you are going to continue straight down it once you have completed your half circle. The most common error with this figure is to make the first half-circle too big

and overshoot the centre line; as you ride the first half-circle don't even *think* about the second one until you are safely *on* the centre line.

6. As his nose meets the centre line one or two strides before X (if you have ridden the first half-circle correctly), straighten your shoulders and think about riding straight ahead, down the centre line. You should make one or two strides with his body *absolutely straight* as you pass over X.

7. As you pass over X start to vibrate your right rein and use a gentle squeeze of your right lower leg to start the new bend, and then turn your shoulders *smoothly and without hurrying* towards the right to begin the second half-circle. Put a little more weight into your right seat bone, but take care not to *lean* to the right or to turn too sharply or else he will fall towards the new direction and your half-circle will be too flat. Again, ride *forward* around the curve and don't be in a rush to get to E.

8. Finally, around two strides before E prepare him for the trot transition by slightly activating him – in other words warn him with small lower leg squeezes that something new is coming.

In Trot

The pattern and preparation are exactly the same as above, the only thing extra that you must handle is that if you are in rising trot, you must change diagonal as you pass over X, and the extra care you must take of his balance in the higher gait.

PRESENTATION

1. Ride the first half-circle as above.

2. As you ride the first of your straight strides, either just before or directly over X, change your diagonal. *Do not* leave your diagonal change until you start your second half-circle: it is part of your warning to him that you are about to ask him to bend and turn in a new direction.

3. *Take time though your change of direction:* ride up to four straight strides on the centre line before turning away onto your second half-circle. Three strides is best, but the worst thing that you can do in this movement is to hurry the change of direction because you will throw him off balance, possibly causing stiffening, resistance and changes of speed.

4. Take great care not to lean over to the new direction as this will also pull him off balance and potentially flatten the shape of the half-circle and/or cause him to rush.

TROUBLESHOOTING

'Lacking activity/needs to be more active'; 'losing energy/impulsion'

Any variation on this theme means:

- In walk, you need to keep him to a quicker, more marching speed and so think of the walk in terms of being a march: brisk and positive. Ask him to walk more briskly by using your leg aids alternately left/right (this tells him to walk, as opposed to breaking into trot), and keep applying them at the speed that *you* want, not the one he offers, i.e. if he slows down, make your aids quicker. *Do not use stronger aids* as this will suggest to him to lengthen his steps and make a bigger ground-covering stride, which is not what you want.

- In trot you must also aid at your own speed instead of matching him: trotting on small circles needs quite a bit of effort and you may find him slowing down, especially on the second half-circle, so monitor his tempo and keep him up to speed.

'Falling in on first/second half-circle'; 'losing/lacking inside bend on first/second half-circle'

On the surface these may seem to be different problems but both stem from a horse's natural crookedness, with a tendency for him to fall towards one shoulder, and in the extreme case to lose his inside bend.

You should know from your home schooling which side he falls towards, so that when you ride the half-circle with that particular shoulder on the *inside* of the shape, pre-empt his falling inward by deliberately riding the shape deeper. Despite your good intentions it is unlikely that he will actually perform the half-circle to your intended shape, and his tendency to drift inward will reduce the figure to the correct size.

Make sure that you sit up straight, and do not lean to the inside yourself: if your weight is excessively to one side you will pull him off balance and make the problem worse.

If inside bend is also an issue, riding the half-circle deep, as described, will also keep him more upright and balanced, and give both you and he a better opportunity to find an inside bend. Make sure that you are turning your body sufficiently to ask him for an inside bend, and in the short term if necessary, take your inside rein inward to his withers to push his shoulders to the outside of the figure. This is, of course, only a short-term solution for the day of your competition; in the long term you need to work more on his suppleness and balance at home.

'Falling out on first/second half-circle'; 'too much neck bend on first/second half-circle'

This is the opposite problem to the one directly above and occurs when the shoulder towards which he naturally drifts is on the *outside* of one of the half-circles.

Here you must make more use of your outside rein, turning your upper body (outside shoulder forward) with your elbow closed tightly in against your ribcage and the knuckles of your outside hand literally pushing inward against his crest (see the photograph on page 123). The direction for your outside hand should be clearly towards his inside ear, and the tighter you close your elbow, the greater control you will exert over his outside shoulder.

Check also your own weight distribution: if you have slipped (or he has pushed you) towards the outside of the saddle, your weight will be dragging him outward. Even if you have not budged, you may need (in the short-term) to exaggerate your weight to the inside to counteract his tendency to drift outward. Take care to do this *without* leaning your upper body to the inside.

'Stiffened/hollowed/lost balance over X'

If your horse is genuinely supple enough to manage this change of direction, then you probably hurried him through the process. Any change of direction challenges both his suppleness and his balance and will also show any differences in his acceptance of the bit on the two sides of his mouth. Next time:

- Take greater care about the speed at which you ask him to change from one bend to the other: take several strides to accomplish this.

- Ensure that you are sitting upright, turning your shoulders from one side to the other and not *leaning over* suddenly and pulling him off balance.

- Check that your contact has a soft, forward direction and that you are not drawing backward which will result in him stiffening his back and hind legs.

- Take time and ask for the flexion change with soft vibrations on the new inside rein; sudden or overly-strong hand aids may cause justifiable resistance.

15 Turning Across the School

These turns may be performed in walk, trot or canter. In canter, the movement incorporates a simple change when crossing the centre line and will be dealt with in Chapter 26.

Example
'CMB working trot; B turn right; E track left; EKA working trot.'

Turning across the school from right to left.

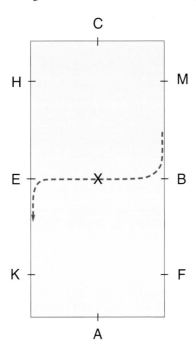

WHAT THE JUDGE WANTS TO SEE

- A rhythmic, active gait and a steady round outline, all of which should remain constant throughout the movement.

- A balanced and supple turn of 90 degrees away from the track (one quarter of a small circle, as in the corners of the school) that begins before the marker, shows clear inside bend from your horse's nose to his tail, and finishes by straightening onto a straight line that is at right angles to the track and directly facing the opposite marker.

- A clear straight line for several metres heading directly towards the opposite marker before the next turn begins.

- A second turn with the same qualities as the first, showing an equal suppleness in the new direction as that shown in the first turn.

- No resistance, stiffening, leaning over to the side or swinging of the quarters during the turns.

PREPARATION

1. As you approach the first turn, ensure that you have your horse moving in the best impulsion (without speed) and balance that he can produce. If you feel that he is travelling a touch too quickly or is not in good balance, then make a half-halt at least two strides before you intend to start your turn. Try to make your aids as small as possible (whilst still achieving your desired result) as you do not want to cause him to stiffen or hollow just prior to the turn.

2. About two strides before your turn, start to ask him for a flexion to (in the above example) the right by softly vibrating the inside rein. This both warns him that you are about to turn away from the track, and starts him producing the bend that he will need to make the turn smoothly and well.

PRESENTATION

1. From practice at home you should know how far before B you will need to start turning to have your horse clearly on the line between B and E. This will depend on such things as his suppleness, his balance and his reaction time, and possibly his sheer size! With this knowledge in mind try to turn as near to the marker as you can without being too ambitious, but take care not to leave it until too late (see the diagrams opposite for the result of either of these miscalculations).

2. Make your turn by turning your upper body to the right and putting a little more weight into your inside seat bone and stirrup. Take care not to lean your upper body to the side or to shift your weight too suddenly or else you may pull your horse off balance. He should remain upright during the turn, with a bend throughout his body length.

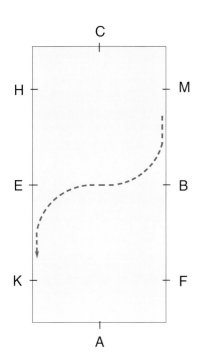
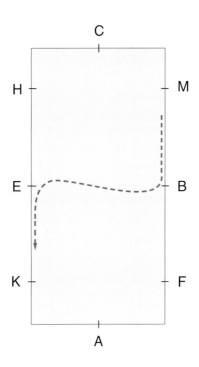

Turning too wide and too late. (*Left*) These turns are too wide, showing very little in the way of straight strides on the E–B line; not what the judge wants to see! (*Right*) The first turn was started too late and then overcorrected, which is a common error.

3. Use your inside leg at the girth at a constant speed, but with a little more strength to encourage him to bend and to maintain his speed and impulsion. As discussed under 10 m circles, a tighter arc is more demanding in terms of impulsion and he may try to either slow down or to leave his hind legs out behind himself.

4. Straighten onto the B-E line by straightening your shoulders until your face and body are directly facing towards E, and equalise the weight in your two seat bones and stirrups.

5. If you are in rising trot change your diagonal as you pass over X. This will be the horse's first indicator that he is going to be asked to turn in the opposite direction and gives him time to start organising his body to produce the bend.

6. At the appropriate distance before E, start your left turn using the aids already described, but the opposite way around. Again, do not turn either too early or too late: practice, practice.

7. Ride away from E in the same tempo and outline as you had before you began the movement.

TROUBLESHOOTING

'Came above bit in turns'

Unless you have an ongoing problem with your horse's outline, the most likely causes here are that you were too sharp, too strong or too abrupt with your hand aids, or that he lacked/lost balance or impulsion.

Take greater care with your preparation, making certain that you give him plenty of time to respond to **soft** rein aids. Remember to use a half-halt as you approach the marker to improve his balance and engagement, and to use your inside leg as you move through the turns to maintain his impulsion. Ensure also that you do not put your weight too suddenly or too extremely to the side (i.e. don't lean over) or else you may compromise his balance, which might cause him to hollow.

'Leaning over in turns'; 'lost balance in turns'

The possible causes are:

■   Your horse may not be as supple as you think/hope and the only way that he could get around the angle of turn that you demanded was to lean over. Do more suppling and bending work at home, and perhaps ask for a less acute turn in competition until he is better able to comply.

■   You may have shifted your weight too much or too suddenly to the side, pulling him off balance. Sit up straight and make sure that you turn your upper body sufficiently to turn him, with a less dramatic weight shift.

■   You did not have him sufficiently balanced, or he may have been going too fast as you approached the movement, so that he went through the turns a bit like a bicycle, leaning over to the side and possibly also gaining speed. Make a point of half-halting a few steps before reaching the marker.

■   You asked for the turn too late, without sufficient warning and he did the best he could. Always warn him several steps before the marker that you are going to ask him to turn, and plan ahead (know your test) so that you don't find yourself asking him too late. Remember: it takes time for your signals to travel to his brain, be processed, and then travel to his muscles to tell them to respond.

■   He needs to take more responsibility for his own carriage: the moment you feel him starting to lean or drift, ride a feeling of leg-yielding outward; this will push his ribcage upright, putting him into a position where he will have to step underneath himself with his inside hind leg and carry his own body-weight.

'Fell inward'; 'lacked bend'; 'wrong bend' in first/second turn

Your horse will always have a tendency to fall towards one of his shoulders because all horses are born naturally crooked. When he falls towards the shoulder that is on the inside of the bend, he will also lack or lose the bend to that side. In training you should be working towards making his two sides more equal, but in the early days of competition, tension or lack of attention will allow such crookedness to reassert itself.

It is also possible that you failed to either prepare the turn sufficiently well, or that you did not ask for the bend clearly enough (or at all!). Review the sections above on riding this movement, and focus at home on improving his suppleness and balance.

If he still falls in/loses the bend in competition, do the following.

- In the short term (just at a show), use an *indirect rein* (inside rein moves inward to, or even across, the inside shoulder) to re-position his shoulders to the outside of the curve and insist upon inside bend. Just remember that you *must not* do this long term (in training), or he will learn to lean against your rein for support, and perpetuate or even exacerbate the problem.

- Use stronger inside leg aids to insist on inside bend and to improve his impulsion (inside hind leg stepping actively forward beneath his body), as this will help him to better sustain his balance and make him less likely to fall sideways. In extreme cases feel as though you are leg-yielding him outward during the turn.

'Fell out'; 'too much neck bend' in first/second turn

This is the opposite of the above issue, and may be compounded by your steering aids if you either used too much inside rein, or you threw away the outside rein in the turn. Excessive neck bend may be either the cause or the consequence of your horse falling outward. To correct these issues, check:

- That you have turned your upper body enough, with your upper arms close to your ribcage so that your outside hand has moved inward and forward towards your horse's crest, with the outside rein snug against his neck (see the photograph on page 123), and that your inside hand has moved inward towards the direction of bend, but is not pulling backward.

- That you have put a little more weight into your inside seat bone and stirrup, *without* leaning over. If you lean to the inside, your seat will slide towards the outside of the saddle, pulling him outward.

- If he is still falling outward despite the above, then exaggerate your aids: turn your upper body more, press the outside rein even tighter against his neck, and put even more weight to the inside of the saddle. If necessary, even feel like you are pulling your outside elbow backward (as you are probably allowing it too far forward in the first place), and open your inside forearm more to the inside (elbow remains against your ribs) in a feeling of leading him around the turn.

'Speeded up in turns'

This is a loss of balance which may be the horse's alone, or you may be causing it by leaning either forward or to the inside.

■ Make a clear effort to sit up straight and simply turn your upper body from the waist with no leaning in either direction.

■ Make sure to half-halt before each turn, so as to put him in his best balance before asking for the turns.

'Slowed down in turns'; 'lost impulsion in turns'

This issue is covered under Presentation, point 3, on page 153. To prevent or deal with this if it starts to occur during a turn you must first train yourself to be very aware of the tempo so that you notice any slowing, and take care not to change the speed of your leg aids to match him. Keep your aids up to the speed that you require, and slightly increase their strength so that he has to match you, and not the other way around.

'Quarters swung out in turn(s)'

■ You may have made too abrupt or too tight a turn making it impossible for your horse to bend his body around the arc of the curve. Think ahead and plan to turn a bit sooner before the marker to make it easier for him.

■ He may be too stiff for the angle of turn you demanded, indicating that you need to do more work on suppling him at home and, until he improves, in competition ask for a shallower turn, so begin each turn a metre or two sooner.

■ He may be evading the engaging effect of the turn by deliberately swinging his haunches outward. This requires you to *use* some outside leg during the turn, rather than just allowing your outside leg to hang passively in an outside leg position (see the photograph on page 121). As you begin the turn, close your outside leg firmly against his side; if he pushes into it, use it with greater strength until you have a feeling of *almost* riding haunches-in.

'Wobbled before second turn'; 'fell/drifted to right/left before second turn'

These comments mean that you needed to pay more attention to straightening him onto the line between the two turns, or that you did not prepare the second turn – possibly you forgot to change your diagonal – and he was not quite sure which way he was going to be asked to go.

As you are finishing the first turn, fix your eyes on the marker directly ahead of you and fully straighten him onto that line. Change your diagonal as you pass over X and almost immediately start indicating to him which way he is going to turn next by following the instructions outlined above.

16 Free Walk, Medium Walk and Extended Walk

Free walk is included in tests for two reasons:

1. As an opportunity for your horse to relax (mentally and physically) and to stretch his muscles during a test.

2. As proof that he is working in a biomechanically correct way, as this will produce correct stretching when you lengthen the reins.

Free walk may be performed on a number of different patterns: on a long diagonal, a short diagonal, two short diagonals with a V-shaped turn, and on a half 20 m circle.

Medium walk is performed on 10 m half circles, and on straight lines including diagonals. It is also required before and immediately after both free and extended walks, and there may be a mark awarded for the transition from free walk to medium walk. (At higher levels collected walk is required, but this is beyond the scope of this book.)

Extended walk should be ridden much like free walk, with just a little more contact but still allowing him to lower and stretch his head and neck.

Whichever walk you are riding, the most important feature is the clarity of the four-beat sequence for without this it will be marked as 'insufficient', i.e. a 4, or at best, in cases when there is just a hint of loss of sequence, possibly a 5, but never more than this.

WHAT THE JUDGE WANTS TO SEE

- A clear four-beat walk with even spacing (both in time and in length) between the footfalls.

Free walk on a long rein: Stanley has lengthened and lowered his head and neck so that his poll is clearly below his withers. Ideally he should have taken his nose slightly more forward and maintained a little more connection to the contact.

Extended walk: even though Stanley is stretching well forward and down, he is still clearly on a contact.

- A marching tempo that is energetic, brisk and purposeful without being hurried, showing activity behind and freedom in the shoulders.

- Relaxation and suppleness throughout the horse's frame so that his whole body moves. Picture a big cat like a panther walking, every bit of his body moving with supple freedom; this is how your horse should look.

- Steps that have clear overtrack, i.e. the hind feet touch the ground in front of the footprints of the forefeet. This should be of moderate length in the case of medium walk, and marked in free walk and extended walk.

- In **medium walk**: a consistent soft contact with the bit in an outline that has an arched and rounded but not shortened top line.

A pleasing outline in medium walk.

- In **free walk**: the reins should be given so that they are long enough for your horse to stretch his neck to its full length with a lowering of his head until (as a minimum) his poll drops below his withers. He should take his nose slightly forward so that his face is in front of the vertical and you should have just enough contact that you can lightly feel his mouth on the other end of the reins.

- In **extended walk** you should also allow him to stretch forward and down (poll below withers) but maintain a little more contact with his mouth than in free walk (see photographs on page 159). He should cover as much ground as possible but without hurrying or losing rhythm.

- Correct alignment to the figure being performed (i.e. straightness on straight lines, appropriate bend on circles, corners and turns).

- Genuine relaxed acceptance of the contact and maintenance of impulsion during the transition from free or extended walk to medium walk.

PREPARATION

Try to ride your best transition from the previous gait into medium walk, asking him to take more weight onto his haunches (see Chapter 8). As soon as you are in medium walk, relax and swing along with your seat, and *slightly* follow his head motion with your hands (i.e. not 'rowing' with a big movement). You should not need to adjust your rein length but, if he is a little tense, you could lengthen them, again *very slightly*, to help him to feel more freedom.

If he is a little lazy, keep him up to tempo by using your legs alternately at the speed that *you* desire, not the one that he offers. Some tests require quite a distance in medium walk and so achieving a walk that is both relaxed yet purposeful as quickly as you can after a transition is an important habit to develop.

Transition to Free/Extended Walk

1. Open your fingers and allow the horse to take the reins.

2. Follow the increased nodding motion of his head with your hands making sure that the direction of their movement is towards where his mouth *should* be (i.e. forward and down), and not necessarily where his mouth *is*. If he is unsure about lowering his head and neck this will encourage him to do so.

3. Increase the size (but not the speed) of your seat movement in the saddle to encourage him to lengthen his strides.

4. With some horses, a slight forward incline of your upper body (from the hips) to lighten your seat may encourage a more relaxed back and so improve the lengthening of both his frame and steps; with others this might encourage jogging and you will need to sit upright with your weight fully in the saddle. Experiment and see which works best for you.

When you ride free walk, take care that *your hands move in a forward direction* throughout the movement. Despite the length of your reins, your horse will still

Inclining slightly forward from the hips, with a straight back to lighten my seat and encourage relaxation and lengthening of Stanley's frame and steps.

feel the *direction* of your contact, i.e. a long rein does not necessarily make for a forward-feeling contact.

I belabour this point because, as a judge, I have often seen riders restricting their horses in free walk *despite* having a long rein, because their hands were not pushed sufficiently forward.

Turning in Free Walk

Example
'KB change the rein in free walk on a long rein; BH change the rein in free walk on a long rein; H medium walk.'

As your reins are long, your aiding for the turn must come primarily from your body positioning. In the above example, as you approach B start to turn your shoulders towards the left and put a little more weight into your left (inside) seat bone by drawing your outside leg back from the hip. The horse's body will automatically realign itself beneath you: this is as a result of his natural righting mechanisms and is not a learned response. Also, even with the long reins he will still feel the left rein move slightly to the left, and the right rein come against his shoulder and he will turn accordingly.

Riding free walk on a half 20 m circle is achieved in the same manner.

Turning in free walk: using clear body, weight and leg positioning.

Transition from Free/Extended Walk to Medium Walk

This is often the hardest part of these movements because of nervous anticipation about what is to follow. Frequent practice out of the competition environment will help you to establish a more relaxed approach to this transition by repeating it when you are *not* going to immediately move into trot or canter: try doing it whilst cooling down after a work session, or even out on a hack.

1. Begin your transition several steps before the marker: practice will tell you how long it will take to shorten your horse's steps and frame *without* him stiffening or arguing.

2. Start to make a smaller motion with your seat to begin shortening his strides.

3. Shorten your reins gradually, not all in one go: as you shorten *each rein* make sure that he is round before shortening the next one. Think about drawing his nose inward, towards his chest, never allowing him to poke it forward or come above the bit.

4. Keep using your legs (at an appropriate strength) alternately to keep the tempo clear and to maintain his activity.

TROUBLESHOOTING

'Needs to lower head and neck more'; 'needs to stretch down more'

These comments may indicate that:

- The horse lacked attention and wanted to sightsee.

- He was not working on the correct muscles, so did not feel the need to stretch.

- He was tense and anxious.

- He does not understand 'seeking the contact'.

The younger or inexperienced horse is more likely to be prone to anxiety or sightseeing and if given a few outings to become more familiar with the show environment, this situation will rectify itself.

Some horses need to be taught how to follow the contact down, and this should be worked on at home using a forward and downward contact whilst maintaining an active, forward-going walk. You may even need to lean forward (from the hips) initially to lower your hands sufficiently to guide him in the direction of the ground.

Leaning forward to teach stretch in walk: my lighter seat has encouraged Tommy (Tormenta) to lift and swing his back. My hands are pointing forward and down and he has responded by lowering his head and neck, although I will ultimately need him to also take his nose more forward.

You should not lean this far forward in competition, but see also the photograph on page 162.

Determined lack of attention or desire to stretch down indicates a serious flaw in his general way of going, and should be addressed as a priority in your training.

'Behind the vertical'; 'needs to take nose more forward'

This indicates a lack of desire to seek the contact and in some cases may be accompanied by tension and/or lack of forwardness.

As above, this suggests a problem in his general way of going and needs addressing in his schooling. It may be an indicator that his outline has been achieved using draw reins or other gadgets, or even a double bridle before he is ready for one, and is not the genuine result of a horse working happily forward into a soft contact. It is also possible that his bit is too sharp, causing him to lack confidence in the contact.

On the other hand, it may be as a result of extreme tension, and will possibly sort itself out as he becomes more relaxed in the competition environment.

'Needs to cover more ground'; 'should show more overtrack'; 'needs more freedom in the shoulder'

Not all horses are blessed with the biggest of walks, especially those with naturally upright shoulders (cob types) or overlong backs. If this is the case there is only so much that you can do.

1. Take care of the clarity of the four-beat walk sequence so that you gain as big a mark as the horse is physically capable of and…

2. …try walking him over ground poles to see if he can be taught to stretch out just a little more.

If a horse is naturally capable of more and is just not giving it to you, increase the size of your pelvic movement along the saddle and use stronger (but not quicker) alternating leg aids. Make sure also that you have yielded sufficient rein length so that he feels he has enough freedom to step forward.

Tension can also cause tightness and lack of stride length and if this is the reason you must be careful not to push him too much or he may jog; just sit with a very relaxed seat and back muscles and maybe even stroke him on the neck to help him to relax.

'Lateral steps'; 'ambling'; 'poor sequence'; 'losing rhythm'

In walk, this is the most serious and the most difficult of problems. Some horses are more prone to losing their clear four-beat walk than others, but the most likely reason for this to develop is employing too tight a rein contact in walk, causing tensing of his back muscles. For a horse to walk in clear rhythm he must be able to alternately relax each of his two long back muscles (which are found one on either side of his spine and extending from his withers to his pelvis); any form of restriction or tension destroys his ability to coordinate his legs in their natural sequence. Other causes are riders hurrying the walk, or trying to slow it too much.

This problem usually develops during training, so take extreme care never to walk for too long on a contact on a young or weak horse, or to tinker too much with his natural tempo. Once established, it is almost impossible to return an irregular, lateral or ambling walk to a natural rhythm. Exercises that might help are:

- Walking over ground poles.

- Walking in water.

- Walking in lateral positioning, e.g. shoulder-in.

Once the tendency is introduced, all you can really do is to minimise the impact in a test by encouraging complete relaxation and, in medium walk, employing a longer rein than is ideal.

'Hurried'

If he is genuinely hurrying, you must restrain him by sitting more still in the saddle and not following his full motion with your seat, possibly also closing your thighs a little more firmly around the saddle and feeling almost as if you are trying to hold the saddle still. Tone down the following motion of your hands.

Be sure, however, that you are not the cause of his hurried steps in your efforts to find more activity and purpose (see below).

'Lacks energy'; 'needs more purpose'

This is such a common phrase to see on a dressage sheet, and one that must be treated with great care if you are not to ruin your horse's natural walk.

Firstly, analyse *why* his walk lacks purpose before you start trying to correct it. The possibilities are:

- He lacks strength. This will sort itself out as he becomes fitter and under no circumstances should you overpush this walk or you may ruin it for the future.

- He has a very big walk. The bigger the walk, the slower it will feel as there is a greater gap between footfalls. Overpushing a big walk may push him out of balance/natural rhythm, risking damage to his sequence. Try to *slightly quicken* his footfalls by using quicker leg aids, but take care not to push his steps into being any bigger.

- He is lazy/behind your leg. You need to tackle his overall attitude to forwardness at home: hacking, jumping and interval training may all have a place in encouraging him to think more forward. You should also teach him to be quicker off your leg, using lots of transitions and demanding an instant response to your aids. Consider also his general health and feeding.

- He is tense. Sadly, you cannot just tell a horse to relax, and often the really fast, fizzy horses are the ones who don't go forward in free walk. Pushing such a horse will only result in jogging, so if this is your problem, just sit quietly and settle for a 5 or 6, rather than risk a 4 or below, and more problems in the rest of the test as a result of increased anxiety.

If you do find yourself having to prompt his walk in competition, use alternating leg aids at a quicker tempo than he offers you, and swing actively along with your seat, *but*, take great care to feel what is going on beneath you: overpushing is most likely to result in jogging so back off if you feel him becoming tense.

'Tense'; 'jogging'

See above under: 'needs more purpose'.

'Against the hand/hollow to medium walk'

- Did you take up the reins too quickly? Shortening a horse's frame/reins must be done gradually or you risk startling him into tension and hollowing.

- Did you take too strong a contact? If you were too rough with your hands, he has justification for contesting the contact.

- Did you keep him active enough as you picked him up? If his hind legs are too far behind him to support his posture he will be unable to find a round outline.

- Is this a habitual problem? See earlier in this chapter for suggestions of how to develop good habits with regard to this transition.

17 Half-circle and Return to the Track

This movement describes a teardrop shape, with half-circles of either 15 m or 10 m, ridden in trot or canter.

WHAT THE JUDGE WANTS TO SEE

- A trot or canter that maintains the same qualities of the gait (rhythm, tempo, elasticity and impulsion) before, during and after the movement.

- No change in balance or outline either on the half-circle or on the return.

- A soft change of bend to the new direction as the movement is completed.

- An accurately shaped and positioned figure.

Two diagrams of the teardrop shape of half-circle return to track. (*Left*) 10 m, (*right*) 15 m; illustrating the examples on page 169.

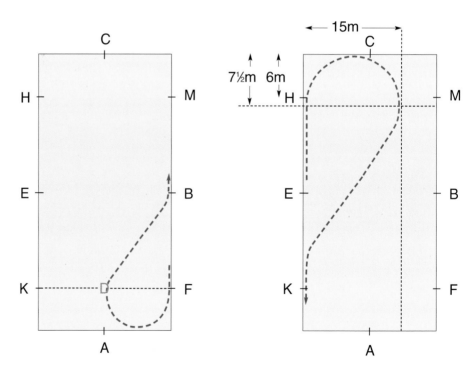

PREPARATION

In both trot and canter, prepare and start your half-circle as described in Chapter 14. For a 10 m half-circle, aim to meet the centre line; for a 15 m half-circle you must estimate the position of the quarter line and aim for that.

PRESENTATION

Once you arrive at either the centre line or the quarter line, turn smoothly but directly onto a straight line towards the marker where the movement finishes. *Do not* straighten onto either the centre line or quarter line first, before heading for the end marker; you should move continuously from the half-circle onto the diagonal line.

Finishing the Movement

Ride the end of the diagonal line that returns to the track just like you would if you were riding across a diagonal of the school to change the rein: aim to reach the track just before the prescribed marker so that by the time *your* body passes the marker, *his* body is fully on the track and straight.

Example

'MBF working trot; FD half-circle right 10 m diameter, returning to the track at B.'

Study this example on the left-hand diagram opposite: you will see that there is no straight section on the centre line before commencing the line from D to B, and this is how you should present this figure.

Start your half-circle at F and *ride it as if you were making a turn onto the centre line*. Although the quarter markers are 6 m from the corners and not 5 m (the radius of your half-circle), if you try to ride the half-circle 1 m short of the track it will almost certainly appear too shallow to the judge.

By the time the horse's nose touches the centre line you should be looking towards B, with your head and upper body turned towards that marker. This will have the effect of starting to turn your horse towards B, so that by the time your own body is above D, he will already be heading towards the track, aiming for *just before* the B marker.

Example

'BAE working canter right; between E & H, half-circle right 15 m diameter returning to the track between E & K; K working trot.'

This figure asks for a short section of counter-canter with a downward transition before the corner. (See Chapter 25 for more details on how to ride counter-canter.)

Although you are given the option of where to start your half-circle, you should aim to start it as late as possible, so that the apex of your half-circle touches the track on the short side (see right-hand diagram on page 168). This will give you the shallowest possible angle of return to the track, which is also the easiest and therefore will look the most fluent to the judge.

Once you have ridden the half-circle, you have two options for riding the return, depending on how well your horse can manage counter-canter:

1. If he finds counter-canter difficult: aim to arrive at the track only a metre or so before K and make your downward transition as his nose reaches the track. In reality this avoids performing counter-canter altogether, but if you succeed in making a balanced downward transition, you can still earn a reasonably high mark.

2. If he finds counter-canter easy: aim to meet the track about halfway between E and K, which will enable you to straighten his body onto the track and show two or three clear strides of counter-canter before making your downward transition.

It is wiser to use the first option above if he tends to become tense or unbalanced in counter-canter, as these issues will affect the quality and ease with which he performs the downward transition.

Example
'PR working canter left; R half-circle left 15 m diameter returning to the track at P; PF counter-canter; F transition to working trot.'

This movement includes a short, straight section of counter-canter on the long side before the transition to trot. Ride this figure as above, aiming to return to the track *just* before P (so that his body is on the track as your body passes P), and maintain the counter-canter with as much balance and engagement as you can.

You will need to practise this movement a few times at home to discover how soon to start preparing the downward transition as this will often be different from the preparation time for a canter/trot transition on an inside lead. It may need longer preparation because the balance is more difficult to achieve, or you may need to leave it until the last possible moment to prevent him from breaking early if he finds counter-canter difficult – trial and error will give you the answer with your own individual.

TROUBLESHOOTING

'Half-circle too big'; 'falling out on half-circle'; 'too much neck bend on half-circle'

See the same subject under: 'Two 10 m half-circles' on page 150.

'Fell in on half-circle'; 'leaning in on half-circle'; lacked bend/balance on half-circle'

See the same subject under: 'Two 10m half-circles' on page 149.

'Lost balance/straightness'; 'falling sideways'

Unless these comments relate to a particular part of the movement, such as the half-circle, they are generally given when your horse wobbles around the figure, drifting one way or another and not producing the crisp, clear-cut figure shown in the diagrams.

Review the instructions on how to ride this shape and pay close attention to aligning his body with first the half-circle and then, without pause, directly onto the straight line. Control of his outside shoulder as you move from curve to straight line is what you need, so keep your outside hand close to his shoulder (see photograph page 123) and as you move onto the straight line be absolutely sure that you have squared your upper body so that his shoulders are straightened onto the line.

'Moving laterally'

This means that on your line of return the horse had his haunches too far to the side and was possibly also crossing his legs, performing an unrequested leg-yield or half-pass.

With more highly trained horses who know these movements, be aware that they quite enjoy producing them and will often offer them even when you don't want them! Again, control of the shoulders is what you need, to keep them clearly and continuously ahead of his haunches so that his spine is totally aligned to your straight line. *Do not* try to push his haunches back into place by taking one leg further back than the other: this is likely to cause fishtailing, when his haunches swing from side to side. Instead, ride more positively forward (stronger but not quicker leg aids) as you come off the half-circle onto the straight line, and be diligent about straightening him as described above, under 'falling sideways'.

18 Serpentines and Loops

Serpentines consist of half-circles connected by straight lines and can be ridden in both trot and canter, the latter with simple changes when crossing the centre line, or with no change of lead (counter-canter).

Depending on the size of the half-circle, the straight connection will vary in length, but you should always be parallel to the short side when you cross the centre line.

Loops are shallow serpentines of between 5 m and 10 m depth. For diagrams and more details, see page 177.

Both figures challenge your horse's balance and suppleness, with at least two changes of bend and direction in each figure.

Serpentines: a) three-loop serpentine in 40 m arena; b) four-loop serpentine in 40 m arena; c) three-loop serpentine in 60 m arena; d) four-loop serpentine in 60 m arena; e) five-loop serpentine in 60 m arena.

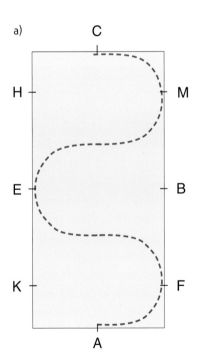

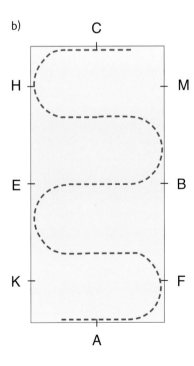

c)

d)

e)

WHAT THE JUDGE WANTS TO SEE

- The same quality of gait before, during and after the serpentine.

- No losses of balance or outline and the same impulsion throughout.

- A supple bend through the horse's body that is equal in both directions.

- No stiffening during the changes of bend.

- Evenly distributed loops of the correct size and shape.

Serpentines

Distribution of Loops

Depending on the number of loops that you are riding, you may or may not have markers to assist you with the distribution of your loops.

Three-loop serpentines
In the 40 m arena
The most common serpentine is the three-loop serpentine in the 40 m arena; unfortunately this is one of the most difficult to judge in terms of loop distribution. Study the diagrams on pages 172 and 173: the only marker that is of any real use is the half-school marker. In example (a) you must touch E at the peak of your second loop, or exactly halfway through your serpentine, after 1½ loops. You need to cross the centre line 13.3 m above A, and again at 13.3 m below C (or vice versa).

Again, practice at home will enable you ultimately to ride this figure without having to think too hard. If you have trouble getting the distribution right to start with, try using cones placed to either side of this point on the centre line, or markers placed on the fence at 13.3 m from the corner (they will be directly in front of you if you are correctly positioned as you cross the centre line), and work with these until you can reproduce the figure without visual aids.

In the 60 m arena
A three-loop serpentine in the 60 m arena is quite simply three 20 m half-circles joined as you cross the centre line, with the barest minimum of a straight section where the half-circles meet; see diagram (c).

Four-loop serpentines
In the 40 m arena
Four-loop serpentines in the short arena consist of four 10 m half-circles joined by

straight lines; see diagram (b). If you have developed a good muscle memory for how a 10 m circle should feel, this will help. You must cross the centre line at a point that is halfway between A and X (10 m from either marker), at X, and again halfway between X and C. You will be exactly halfway through your serpentine (having completed two loops) as you travel across the half-school line between E and B.

In the 60 m arena

This serpentine is made up of four joined 15 m half-circles and so, once again, if your muscle memory for the 15 m circles is established, you will find it easier. The distribution is as for the 40 m arena, although in this case halfway between A and X will be 15 m from either marker, not 10 m; see diagram (d).

Using plastic containers to mark out the correct place to cross the centre line in a serpentine.

Do not try to use the markers R, S, V or P as reference points as their positions are of no help with this figure.

Five-loop serpentines

This serpentine is only required in the 60 m arena. The half-circles are of 12 m, and once again the markers are of little assistance. You need to have completed 2½ loops as you touch the track at either E or B. If you want to lay it out for practice at home, use the suggestions made for the three-loop serpentine above using 12 m measurements to position your markers. Once again: practice makes perfect, or makes it easier at least!

Example

I have picked just one variation of the serpentine, the 3-loop serpentine, as an example because it is the simplest and consequently most commonly seen variation.

'EK working trot; A serpentine 3 loops, each loop to go to the side of the arena finishing at C; CEK working trot.'

PREPARATION

In this example, approach A in the best rhythm, speed and balance that you can manage, if necessary making a half-halt during the preceding corner. At A, start

The Continental serpentine.

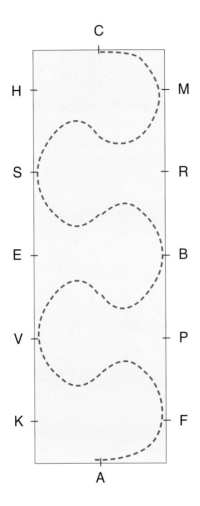

to ask for left bend with soft vibrations on your left rein, turning your shoulders towards the left and pressing your left calf against his ribcage to initiate bend.

PRESENTATION

If you have enough practice under your belt, you should not have to think too hard about the size and shape of the figure. The most important factors to focus on now are having correctly aligned bend to each of the loops, and making smooth, fluent changes from one bend to the next. You will almost certainly find the change of bend easier going in one direction than the other: changing from the horse's stiff side to his hollow side will be easier for both of you as his body naturally wants to lose the one bend and gain the other.

Review riding the change of bend described in Chapter 11, and use the same techniques between each of the loops in the serpentine. With the exception of the three-loop serpentine in the 60 m arena you will have the luxury of a little more time to complete your bend change, courtesy of the connecting straight line between the half-circles.

- *Make sure* that your connecting straight lines are *straight*, and are truly parallel with the short sides of the arena.

- *Do not* ride a Continental serpentine, in which the straight sections loop back on themselves (see diagram above).

- *Do* change your diagonal (if you are rising to the trot) either *one stride before* or, at the latest, *as you cross* the centre line. This warns your horse that you are going to change direction and allows him time to react and to organise his body ready for the new direction.

Loops

Example
The loops in the diagrams below would be variously described as: 'KXH one loop' or 'between K&H one loop 10 m in from track' and 'KH one loop 5 m in from track'.

Your goal is to ride a smooth and evenly distributed loop starting from one quarter marker and finishing at the quarter marker at the other end of the long side.

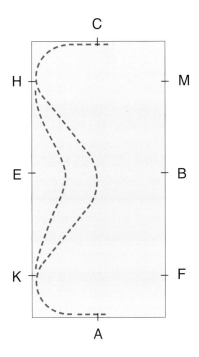

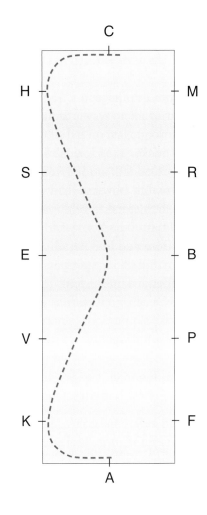

(*Left*) 5 m and 10 m loops in the 40 m arena. (*Right*) 10 m loop in the 60 m arena.

10 m Loops in Trot

PREPARATION

Make a half-halt as you approach the corner preceding your loop, and ride *into* the corner: if your corner is too shallow your loop will be more difficult to ride as you will not leave the track until several metres *after* the quarter marker.

PRESENTATION

1. As you come through this corner, turn your face to look at X (midway between E and B). Allow your upper body to turn with your head, and you will automatically have your hands correctly positioned to ask your horse to both turn and bend.

2. Keep a little more weight in your inside seat bone and stirrup (where it should have been through the corner) to keep him turning out of the corner, instead of straightening onto the long side.

3. Keep your outside rein closed against his outside shoulder (see the photograph on page 123), or he will tend to lean outward and cling to the track.

4. Once he is on the line heading towards X you will need to begin a gradual slight weight change to the other side to start asking for both a change of bend and of direction.

5. In trot, you must change his bend to follow the shape of the figure. In the Example on page 177: leave the corner with a *right* bend heading on a gentle curve towards X. As you approach X ask him to develop a slight *left* bend so that you pass over X with a left bend aligned to your gently curving line. Finally, as you begin heading towards the quarter marker just before the next corner, you must change his bend

Turning out of the corner: Nikki has her weight clearly to the inside, although she could sit up taller and lift her head. Ollie has a good inside bend.

Stanley showing a clear change of bend at the peak of the loop: my upper body has turned to the new direction and my weight has been redistributed to my new inside stirrup, showing a slightly deepened heel.

again until he is in *right* bend as he approaches the corner. The aiding for the bend and direction changes is as described in Chapter 11.

6. As the changes of bend and direction are quite shallow it is *not essential* to change diagonal when riding a loop, although with some horses it can be beneficial. The choice is yours.

7. When you make your second change of direction after passing over X, head for a point just *before* H, so that you are fully on the track as your own body passes the marker.

A 10 m loop performed in trot in a 60 m arena. The diagram shows the loop split into three sections and the black dots show where the changes of bend should begin.

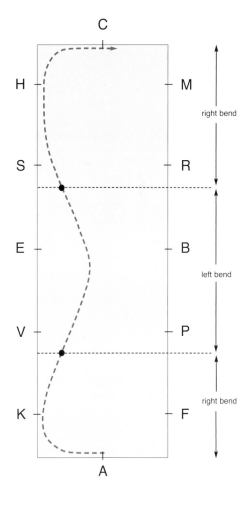

Finishing the Movement

Finish your loop clearly by riding well into the corner. This means you *must* have accomplished point 7 above, which is essential if this figure is to appear smooth and with both a clear start and finish.

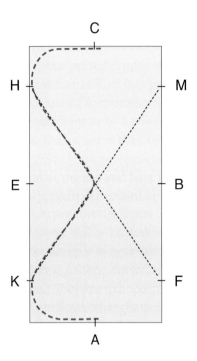

Riding the loop as a V-shape, travelling directly from point to point without the continuous curving of the finished shape. The dotted lines indicate the diagonals.

Developing the Shape of the Figure

If you struggle at first with the shape of this figure, try riding it at home from marker to marker without worrying about the curved shape. Come out of the first corner as if you were riding across the diagonal of the school to change rein, and then when you arrive at X simply change direction to head towards the marker at the end of your figure as shown in the diagram.

When you find that you can ride this accurately, simply start to ride the turns as gentle curves rather than sharp turns and the final figure will develop.

Loops in Canter

Example

'KH one loop 5 metres in from the track.'

The 5 m loop goes only as far into the school as the quarter line and so you will have to estimate a point equidistant between X and E. Alternatively you must estimate 5 m in from the track in front of E, depending on which technique you find works for you. See the left-hand diagram on page 177.

The other major difference from the trot loop described above is that in canter you *must not* change his bend, but maintain it towards his leading leg throughout. This presents a whole new range of challenges, such as how to turn his shoulders (and so change direction) without changing bend (see the photograph on page 219), and how to prevent him from falling back to the track with his weight on his outside shoulder.

This figure is an early introduction to counter-canter on a curved line, and one of the most critical aspects of your aiding will be to maintain *your weight* in the saddle on the side of his leading leg, regardless of the direction in which you are travelling. This subject is covered in more detail in Chapter 25.

TROUBLESHOOTING

'Poorly shaped figure'

This is one of the most common problems with both serpentines and loops and refers most commonly in serpentines to an unequal distribution of loops, and in loops to the riding of straight lines that should not exist.

Review the diagrams and descriptions above and then start practising, preferably with somebody with a degree of experience on the ground to help you by providing feedback on the shapes that you produce.

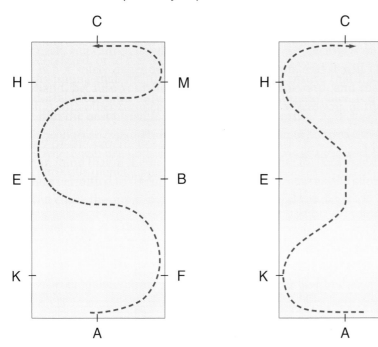

(*Left*) Poorly shaped serpentine with the first two loops too large, leaving little room for the last loop. (*Right*) Poorly shaped loop: the straight section on the centre line should not be there. You should touch the centre line for one stride only at X before curving back towards H.

'Falling in on left/right hand loops', 'wrong bend/lacked bend on left/right hand loops'

These comments all relate to your horse lacking suppleness in one direction, with the knock-on effect that he may also lack balance in that same direction, indicating that more homework is needed to improve his lateral suppleness.

In a test, i.e. a short-term situation, if he falls in or lacks bend (or even refuses to produce inside bend) on, for example, right-hand loops, make sure that you:

■ Are not leaning over to the right and pulling him off balance.

■ Are turning your upper body sufficiently to the right to ask for right-hand bend.

■ Use stronger right-leg squeezes as you change direction to the right to insist that your horse contracts the muscles of his right ribcage (i.e. bends) and keeps his body upright (i.e. stays in balance) as he moves onto the right-hand loop.

■ If necessary, in extreme cases, use an indirect rein, taking your right hand in towards, or even across, his withers to insist that he moves his shoulders outward to the outside of the curve. As soon as you have achieved this, try to lighten your inside rein by moving it back to where it should be (to the right of his shoulders) so that you do not block his inside hind leg from stepping forward. Do not use this correction any more than you have to or else he will start to lean against your hand, making the problem worse in the long run.

'Figure lacked fluency'

This might seem to be a rather vague comment, but it is most likely to be used when either your figure lacked smooth curves and looked a bit jerky, or your changes of direction were less than smooth: either your horse stiffened (or resisted) during the bend changes, or they took too long to complete so that he did not achieve the new bend until partway through the next loop.

When practising at home, try putting a full circle (or two or three) into the peak of each loop.

Ride around each circle as many times as you feel you need to until you have it correctly shaped, and your horse is correctly bent and aligned, before continuing with your serpentine. This can give *you* the feeling of riding really round shapes in the loops, whilst ensuring that your *horse* realises that he will have to remain on the circle until he gives you the correct bend. Riding this pattern a lot will form the habit (in both of you) of always riding correctly shaped loops with the correct bend.

'Stiffening/resisting in changes of bend'

Check that you are not:

■ Asking for the change of bend too abruptly.

■ Pulling back on the new inside rein.

- Throwing your weight from one side to the other too suddenly or too extremely.

Check that you are:

- Starting to use your new inside leg one stride before you cross the centre line to give him time to react to your aids.

- Carefully and smoothly changing your weight distribution from one seat bone and stirrup to the other.

- Turning your upper body smoothly but not too quickly from one side to the other.

If your aiding is correct and your bend changes are still not easy then you must devote more training time to them until he becomes more supple and finds it easier to adjust his musculature from one bend to the other.

You may also find that he accepts the contact more readily on one side of his mouth than on the other. This is usually a reflection of the natural inequality of suppleness that all horses are born with, and all riders must work to improve. A genuine mouth problem is rare, although a rider may create one by hanging onto, or pulling, on one rein, and so if you have this issue, check your own riding first!

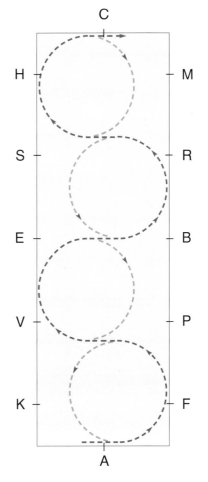

Four-loop serpentine in a 60 m arena with 15 m circles in the peak of each loop.

19 Give and Retake the Reins

This action is required in both trot and canter and is designed to be a test of self-carriage, with nothing altering in your horse's way of going during the brief release of contact. It can be performed on a straight line, on the track or the diagonal of the arena, or at a prescribed position on a circle.

Example

'E circle left 20 m diameter and in second half over centre line give and retake the reins.'

You should push both your hands forward until the contact is clearly released before returning your hands to their normal position, i.e. retake the contact. The movement of your hands should be continuous and the whole thing should take place over two or three strides. It is not a test to see how long you can leave your hands forward, nor should the horse try to move his head forward or down to seek the contact, unlike the movement described as: 'allow the horse to stretch' (see Chapter 20).

Example

'A circle right 15 m and just as returning to A, give and retake the inside rein.'

The object here is to show that you are neither holding your horse into an outline or a bend solely with your hands: if your outside rein contact is too strong, when you release the inside rein your horse will change bend.

WHAT THE JUDGE WANTS TO SEE

- No changes in his outline or bend, i.e. showing that he is not held in place just by your reins.

- A degree of self-carriage, i.e. showing that he is not totally reliant on the reins for his balance and is able to maintain constant rhythm, tempo and carriage.

- No change in his level of engagement, or the suppleness of his back.

- No loss of alignment to the figure, i.e. no swinging or sudden crookedness, or increase in an existing crookedness.

- A soft and willing acceptance of the return to contact with, again, no changes in any of the above features.

PREPARATION

1. At least four or five strides before you reach the place where you will give the reins forward, organise your horse into his best possible balance, rhythm and outline using half-halts.

2. Check, and if necessary correct, his alignment (correct tracking/straightness) to your figure.

3. During the last few strides before your contact release make a couple of mini-releases, each one during just one stride: tiny, quick movements of your hands forward enough to lose any weight in your contact. Make these actions so small that the judge does not see them but clear enough that your horse can feel them. This will help him to be mentally prepared for the total loss of contact, which will not then come as a complete surprise.

PRESENTATION

1. Gradually and smoothly (take care not to startle your horse) push your hand(s) forward towards his mouth. *Do not* raise them to shoulder height (arms parallel to the ground) as you push them forward: this does not achieve contact release.

2. Sit up tall: any tipping forward will put your weight over his shoulders and push him onto his forehand, which may result in him changing his outline or speed.

3. Keep the movement of your seat the same throughout, whether in rising or sitting trot, or canter. Any variation will disturb his rhythm and potentially cause a loss of confidence and/or balance, resulting in him lifting his head up.

4. As soon as you have a achieved a clear release of contact where your rein(s) will have fallen into slack loops and you have no weight in your hand(s), move your hand(s) gradually and smoothly back to their normal position. Take care to reconnect to his mouth softly: an abrupt retake may cause (justifiable) resistance and/or variations to his balance and rhythm.

5. Continue along your figure and start preparing for the next movement in your test.

(*Top*) Correct release of both reins. (*Bottom*) An incorrect attempt at contact release: my hands are too high and as a consequence I still have a contact.

TROUBLESHOOTING

'Came above the bit'; 'lost the outline'; 'hollowed'

Did you make sufficient preparation? Unless you have a problem with keeping him in an outline generally, the most likely reasons for a horse to come above the bit when the contact is released are:

- He had lost balance before you released the contact: either towards one shoulder, or onto his forehand.

- He lacked alignment to your figure (either circle or straight line), and his lack of straightness pulled him off balance when you released the contact.

- You startled him by yielding the contact abruptly.

- He lost attention.

Once you have identified one of the above issues as the culprit, pay particular attention to it during your preparation next time.

- Frequent use of half-halts as you approach the movement will help to improve your horse's balance.

- Pay more particular attention to his straightness in training and learn 1) when he falls onto an outside shoulder, how to place his shoulders in front of his haunches (shoulder-fore), and 2) when he falls onto his inside shoulder, how to produce a feeling of leg-yielding outward, and use these techniques prior to your contact release.

- Make your preparatory mini-releases a little more obvious to him in the steps before the movement.

- Ensure that you have his full attention, using either several small vibrations on your inside rein, or several small taps with your inside leg prior to the release.

'Dropped his head down'; 'fell onto his forehand'.

There are three likely reasons for the above comments:

1. You did not have your horse in a good enough balance before the movement.

2. He tends to work in too deep an outline anyway and took advantage of the lack of contact to drop even deeper.

3. You took too long before regaining the contact and he went to look for it.

The problems in points 1 and 2 can be improved with the use of half-halts during your preparation: try to find the feeling that he is in a trot or canter from which you could easily pop over a small fence, or that you are riding up a hill. If the movement is on a circle, use the first half of the circle to achieve this. If it is on a straight line, you should try to achieve this as you come through the preceding corner: altering his balance is easier on a curve than on a straight line.

Specifically if he tends to work too deep, make a few small upward half-halts, i.e. in the moment of aiding the half-halt, you also momentarily move your fists slightly upward, this action coming largely from your wrists, not your whole forearm (see my book *The Building Blocks of Training*, [J.A. Allen] Chapter 10, TROUBLESHOOTING, for issues about outline), and ensure that he is genuinely in front of your leg, i.e. not slowing down if you cease to aid with your legs. You might want to give him a few quick reminders with a couple of slightly sharper leg aids before you get into the movement.

If you are too slow retaking the reins he might justifiably confuse this movement with 'allow him to stretch'. Whilst making sure not to retake the contact too abruptly, remember that the directive is for this movement to happen over 'two or three strides', and not more. Do not try to be clever and leave your hands forward for four or five strides: this will not gain you any extra marks.

'Gained speed'; 'running'

1. The horse either: lost balance onto his forehand, or…

2. …lost balance laterally due to lack of straightness.

3. You are controlling his speed with your hands, not your seat.

To correct either point 1 or 2, see under: 'dropped his head down' in the section above.

If you are controlling a horse's speed with your reins, then you need to do a bit of retraining to solve this issue. Control of speed and length of stride must be achieved with your *seat*. This involves having a deep enough seat with your upper leg in close contact with the saddle (achieved by a degree of tone in the muscles, not by gripping) and a flexible lower back to allow you to absorb and influence his motion.

If this sounds a bit complicated, think of it in these terms: you need to stay glued to your saddle and move your seat *at your own speed*, not his. Ask yourself: 'is this my trot (or canter), or is it his?' It *must be yours*.

This can also be achieved in rising trot using a degree of closure of your upper legs and knees, without gripping. Gripping involves extreme clenching of the muscles and usually includes the buttock muscles which should *never* be tightened when riding. Imagine that you are holding the *saddle* to your choice of speed, and rise at your own speed, not just following the speed he offers you. If this results in you being slightly out of synchronisation with him, so be it. It is up to him to change his speed to match yours, not the other way around. Place your seat firmly in the saddle each time you sit and imprint *your* rhythm into that saddle!

Pay particular attention to this as you approach a give and retake, and be very pedantic about him listening to your seat.

'Fell in/out'

As described above under 'came above the bit', this will be due to an initial lack of alignment to your figure, and as a result of your horse's natural crookedness. Review the corrective work described above.

'Lost bend'

This shows that you were relying on your hands to create the bend; you must make certain that your horse understands to move his ribcage away from your inside leg, and you must *use* your inside leg!

Prior to an *inside* rein release, prepare as described above, with mini-releases of both rein contacts, and then be very light in your outside contact when you release your inside rein, supporting it with a clear inside leg aid. If necessary, use a feeling of leg-yielding outward throughout the inside rein release.

'Lost attention'

This can happen: something outside the arena may distract your horse at just the wrong moment. If this is not a recurring problem do not be too concerned about an isolated incident.

If it *is* a regular occurrence, you need to work more in your training on his balance, confidence and submission, all of which are tied up with attention to his rider. This relates to his natural instincts. A horse in the wild is most confident when he knows clearly his place in the herd hierarchy, where dominance is denoted by levels of attention accorded to other members of the herd, with the most dominant horse being the one to whom the others pay most attention. You need to take the place of that dominant partner by demanding his attention at all times, and then he will have confidence in you (as his herd leader) and will leave it up to you to look around for potential problems (predators) in the environment, feeling no need to do so for himself.

20 Allow the Horse to Stretch

This action is performed both in trot and canter on a 20 m circle and requires your horse to do the same as he does in free walk on a long rein, i.e. to take his neck forward and down to seek the bit, stretching his neck out whilst remaining relatively round (taking his nose slightly forward but not poking it out), and lowering his poll below his withers.

This movement is designed to show the judge that your horse's outline is genuine and achieved in a correct manner, with the horse seeking the contact and not being held artificially in place with your reins.

WHAT THE JUDGE WANTS TO SEE

- A gradual lengthening of the reins with a consequent lowering and stretching of your horse's neck as he seeks the contact. There should always be a light contact, even when your reins are at their greatest length.

Allowing the horse to stretch in trot: Stanley's poll is below his withers and his frame has lengthened. The rein is not loose, but long and with a light contact.

- Maintenance of his gait in terms of rhythm, tempo and elasticity.

- No change in his balance.

- Unchanged levels of impulsion and suppleness of his back.

- A smooth and easy return to working carriage, with no resistance, stiffening or loss of quality of the gait.

PREPARATION

The three important features of your preparation are to have him:

1. Moving at a steady rhythm (use of half-halts).

2. As balanced as possible (use of half-halts).

3. As relaxed as possible.

PRESENTATION

1. Sit tall and quietly, and aid only as much as you need to with leg and seat to maintain your horse's impulsion.

2. Open your fingers and allow him to take the rein forward and down. Keep your hands quite low and have a forward feel to your contact, easing your hands forward *a little* towards his mouth.

3. You should aim to leave him stretched for a minimum of around a half dozen steps in trot, and about four strides in canter.

4. Shorten your reins gradually, at each stage making sure that he is staying round and accepting the contact softly before you shorten the next rein; you may need to do this over several strides, so don't leave it too late to start.

5. Monitor his tempo and impulsion, and use your seat and/or legs to maintain a constant gait.

An interesting point to note here is that judges often see a marked *improvement* in the quality of a horse's gait during the stretched section of the circle – a point that should say a lot to the rider about their contact, i.e. that it is usually too tight or strong and thus restricting the gaits, but a point which seems to go over the tops of many people's heads!

TROUBLESHOOTING

'Not stretching down/seeking the contact'

There are several reasons why a horse might not stretch:

- His basic outline and throughness need to be more genuine: a horse will only *need* to stretch down if he has used his musculature correctly through the rest of the test – more homework needed on genuine submission and correct connection from leg to hand.

- His balance was too much on the forehand for him to feel comfortable and capable of lowering his neck whilst in motion – take more care with the half-halts in preparation.

- You gave the contact away too abruptly and startled him – this should be a *gradual* lengthening of the reins, not a sudden abandonment.

- He was anxious/tense – this might be because he was unbalanced and/or too fast as you approached the movement (use more half-halts), or he is still not comfortable in a competition environment and needs more mileage.

'Fell onto forehand'; 'running'

Make a point of riding several half-halts during the first few strides of the circle *before* you lengthen your reins to help your horse achieve his best balance. If he still has a problem, then try to ride the circle a little slower and/or underpowered for the moment until his self-carriage is better. Check also that you do not lean forward when you lengthen the reins: putting your weight over his shoulders will cause both of these problems.

'Losing the shape of the circle'; 'falling in/out'

These are crookedness and/or balance issues that will improve with general schooling. The more attention you pay to balancing (half-halts) and aligning a horse to the figure *before* lengthening the reins, the better chance you have of his maintaining both features for the few strides that he is without your rein support.

The other consideration is your own body position: if you are at all crooked or you lean over to one side of the circle, you may well pull him off balance, so sit up and turn your upper body: do not ride your horse as if he is a motorbike!

21 Medium Trot/Canter – Lengthening the Strides

Medium (or lengthened) strides are ridden at trot and canter and may be performed on a diagonal, on a long side, and either on a half or a full 20 m circle. At the early levels you need only produce a few of these strides between the given markers; as you progress up the levels you will need to ride them from marker to marker with clear transitions at start and finish.

THE JUDGE WANTS TO SEE

For 'a few medium/lengthened strides':

- A smooth and gradual increase in the length of strides with no increase in tempo, i.e. the speed of the rhythm.

- The longer strides sustained for half a dozen steps or so, ideally placed evenly on either side of the midpoint of your line which may be on a diagonal, a long side, or a 20 m half-circle. On a full 20 m circle the longer strides should ideally cover around half of the circle.

- A gradual return to working-stride length.

- A consistently maintained balance, i.e. with the horse not falling onto his forehand.

- A *slight* lengthening of the horse's top line with a *slight* lowering of his head and neck during the medium strides, but with no loss of roundness.

For medium strides from marker to marker:

- A clear transition from a working (or collected) gait to medium strides at the start of the movement.

- Sustained strides of the same length throughout the movement, i.e. not fading towards the end.

- Maintenance of the rhythm, tempo and suspension.

- Balance and outline as above.

- A clear transition back to a working (or collected) gait at the end of the movement with no resistance or stiffening of the frame, and no hurried steps.

Medium trot clearly showing longer strides, with Tommy's hind hoof about to overtrack the print of his forefoot. Ideally he could be slightly longer in his neck frame. Tormenta (Spanish x Warmblood) competing with the author at elementary level.

Photograph by Andrew Gilham.

PREPARATION

- As you approach this movement you need to increase your horse's impulsion. Do this with stronger (but not quicker) squeezes of your lower legs whilst restraining slightly with your contact and maintaining the speed of your seat movement (using the muscles around your pelvis to regulate the swing of your seat) so that he doesn't become faster or cover more ground (yet). You should arrive at the place you want to begin lengthening with him eager to go so that all you have to do is to *allow* the lengthening, not create it.

- Be sure to have him *really* round before you start: there is no point trying to lengthen with a hollow horse as his strides will become hurried and, as a consequence, shorter rather than longer.

- Always ensure that your horse is *straight* before allowing lengthening. Any crookedness will cause the thrust from his hindquarters to push unequally towards one shoulder, resulting in a loss of rhythm or a change of gait, e.g. from trot to canter. In canter ensure that he is 'functionally straight', with his two inside legs aligned (slight shoulder-fore positioning), or else he will travel haunches-in resulting in loss of thrust and a deduction of marks for crookedness.

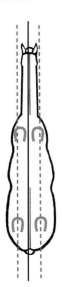 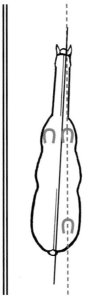

Straightness and functional straightness. (*Left*) The straight horse: note that as his shoulders are narrower than his haunches, his forefeet are closer together than his hind feet. (*Right*) Functional straightness in canter: here both inside hooves are on the same line, i.e. parallel to the track.

PRESENTATION

Lengthened Strides

You have two options for how you approach 'show a few medium strides', and your choice will depend on which one your individual horse finds easiest.

Not all horses are suited to **gradual development** of the medium strides. Some find it easier to produce them from a **clear transition** at the start. In this case, unless he can maintain the medium strides for a long period, you will not be able to position them ideally on either side of your midpoint, but will have your best strides early on, almost directly out of the preceding turn. If this is how your horse produces his best medium strides it is better to do this than to try to show gradual development and an even spread over the required pattern, but with not such good medium strides.

The *quality* of the work that you produce is always more important than the positioning. Obviously, if you can produce good strides in the ideal manner described above, you will get the highest marks, but production of good quality strides, *however positioned*, can still gain a good mark.

Gradual development of medium strides

Prepare as described above, and then once settled onto your line gradually increase the size of your seat swing:

- In *rising trot*, swing your hips up higher and further forward in each stride (but not faster) until you have maximum length of stride, then gradually reduce the size of your rising to reduce the size of his strides.

- In *sitting trot*, gradually press your seat in a longer (but not quicker) horizontal motion from the back to the front of the saddle. You must keep your buttock muscles relaxed to allow your seat to stay adhesively attached to the saddle, and use your deep stomach and lower back muscles to produce this larger motion. To reduce the stride length, gradually reduce the size of your seat action; this may also involve the use of some toning of your inner thigh (adductor) muscles, though not enough to push you away from the saddle (gripping), and must be done without tensing the buttock muscles. Do *not* pull on the reins – this will only cause him to stiffen and make the whole experience difficult and uncomfortable, but *do* keep using your lower legs to keep him stepping under his body with his hind legs.

- In *canter*, use the same increase in seat action as in sitting trot, though always with your inside seat bone remaining in advance of your outside seat bone (outside leg slightly drawn back from the hip to maintain this position), to ensure that he understands clearly to remain on the same canter lead. Return to working strides as for sitting trot, and take care to be soft with your rein contact or else he may break to the trot.

Medium strides from a clear transition

The preparation and production of the medium strides (and the gradual transition back to working) is as described above, but instead of a gradual increase in the size of your seat action, change it directly to the bigger movement as you leave the turn preceding the movement. This is particularly appropriate for horses who tend to lose their balance towards their forehand on straight lines; in other words, use the preceding turn to increase your horse's engagement, then harness it before he has a chance to lose it. Once you feel his balance beginning to go, reduce the stride length before he can begin to run. With practice you will be able to increase the number of strides that he can achieve before his balance starts to go towards his shoulders, until eventually you can maintain them for the full length of the pattern.

If your horse *can* produce medium strides for the whole length of the pattern without loss of balance, then show them. Once you move up to the next level you will need to show this and, if your horse is capable, you should not be penalised for showing 'too much'. Modern judge training is geared towards recognising the quality of your work, not nit-picking about accuracy.

Your *rein contact* during medium strides must allow for a *slight* lengthening of his frame, by easing your hands forward just a small amount to encourage him to lengthen and lower his neck frame: his whole outline during medium gaits must be slightly longer. On the other hand, take care not to throw your reins away as this will drop him onto his forehand and cause him to lose confidence in you: in the earlier stages he will still need a little support from your reins to help with his balance.

As you reduce his strides back to working length, take care not to move your hands backward too suddenly, only moving them as *his* outline shortens, not using them as a tool with which to shorten his neck, which would cause him to stiffen his back and lose rather than gain impulsion/engagement.

Medium Strides from Marker to Marker

The preparation and riding of the medium strides, plus the transition at the start are as described above. You must then maintain the medium strides until you are within a few strides of the end marker and then ride a clear transition back to the working/collected gait by doing the following.

- Increase the tone in your upper body muscles so that you cease to follow his bigger movement and change the action of your seat from a large horizontal swing to a shorter, more vertical movement to encourage him to lift his back and spring upward more, i.e. collect.

- Close your lower legs on his belly: he should bring his hind legs more forward beneath his body to take the weight, not drop onto his shoulders and reduce the stride length by bracing his front legs.

- Make soft half-halts with your fingers, but *do not* pull backward or tense your forearms as this will cause him to stiffen and possibly to resist. If he genuinely understands and is physically capable of obeying your seat and legs, your hands should have little or nothing to do in this transition.

TROUBLESHOOTING

In Medium/Lengthened Trot Strides

'Running instead of lengthening'

Think about how you ask your horse to lengthen his strides. Do you:

- Prepare him sufficiently by increasing impulsion (but not speed) in the corner preceding the movement? If he doesn't have his hind legs active and well enough engaged under his body he has no pushing power and he will only be able to rush, not lengthen. Create this impulsion by squeezing with a stronger leg and use an increase in the muscle tone in your torso so that your seat pressure increases when you sit into the saddle, but *without* increasing the *speed* of your aids. Contain the impulsion with a slight feeling of restraint in your contact until you are ready to allow the lengthening.

■ Create lengthening by trying to kick him into it? You must be clear – your *legs* create impulsion, but your *seat* controls the length of his strides. Kicking him harder and/or faster will only cause him to stiffen his body and move his legs more quickly. See above for descriptions of how to use your seat in each gait.

If you are asking your horse correctly and he still runs, then consider:

■ Does he *understand* what you are asking? Some horses lengthen naturally; others need to be taught. You may need to backtrack and do more training at home before he will produce medium strides in competition.

■ Does his conformation permit lengthening? Not all horses are physically capable of lengthening and no amount of training will solve that. If he genuinely cannot lengthen his strides, then just ride him in a consistent rhythm and outline: this is preferable to making him run.

■ Has he been rushed in the past and, as a result, is anxious about being asked for medium strides? In this case you will need to be very clear with your seat, moving it determinedly at the speed that you want, not the one that *he* wants. You may even need to close your knees and thighs more firmly against the saddle and try to make the *saddle* move at your chosen speed – your horse will slow down to match his saddle! This process may take you many months before he will conform to your seat actions easily, but it *is* possible to retrain this type of problem.

'Lost rhythm'; 'broke'; 'cantered'

Check your horse's *straightness*. You probably did not have him quite straight enough before you asked for medium strides (see above under Preparation). You will find him easier to straighten in one direction than the other owing to his natural crookedness. When turning into the movement with his hollow (more easily bent) side on the *inside* you are more likely to have this problem, as his weight will drift towards his outside shoulder.

In *rising trot* you may find him easier to straighten if you change your diagonal during the turn before the movement, rather than at the end of it. Experiment with this: some horses are better if you change diagonals at the beginning in both directions; some need you to change at the beginning in one direction and at the end in the other.

If straightness is not the answer, you may be looking at a slight restriction in the movement of one shoulder/forelimb, or unequal power from one hind limb, either of which may prove to be a veterinary issue. Tension or excitement may also be causes, as can over-riding, or asking for more than he can yet achieve and still remain in balance. Try to determine the cause and possibly put him under less pressure for a few competitions until he is better able to cope, both physically and mentally.

'Fell onto his forehand and cantered'; 'ran into canter'

Did you:

- Push your horse beyond his point of balance at his current stage of training? Try asking for a little less until he is stronger/better balanced.

- Drop him onto his forehand by throwing away your contact? Although you must allow his outline to lengthen *slightly*, you must not drop the contact entirely; at this stage of his career he still needs a degree of support from your reins to help him maintain his balance; self-carriage takes time to develop.

- Drop him onto his forehand by leaning forward? Sit up tall, or even think about leaning slightly back until you no longer tip forward.

- Throw him at it with everything you have? Using excessive leg and/or seat can push his weight forward onto his shoulders; be a little quieter in your aiding.

- Lack preparation, so you began with his hind legs insufficiently beneath him to support the longer strides? Review the section above on preparation, including attention to straightness.

Are you certain that your horse has had sufficient training at home, so that he both understands what you are asking, and has the physical strength to perform this movement?

It is also likely that he may lose his balance in this manner because of previous experience, of being asked to perform medium strides before he was ready to do so, causing the pattern to be set in his memory that this is what is required of him in competition. If this is the case, you must take the time when competing to ask only for the barest minimum of lengthening, not allowing him to throw his weight forward, and build up to bigger strides again over a period of months. For this you will need to accept that you will gain a low mark in the short term, in the knowledge that you are fixing this for the future.

'Stiffened'; 'hollowed'

These problems can result from a number of causes:

- Your horse's outline was not sufficiently round before you asked for lengthening, or is not yet secure in his general work.

- He is not yet well balanced or strong enough to manage medium strides with confidence.

- You startled him by aiding too suddenly.

- You asked more of him then he is yet able to produce.

- You kept the rein contact too short/tight or threw it away so that he felt abandoned.

Try to determine which of these is the cause and address it by reviewing the instructions above on how to produce medium strides correctly. Bear in mind that a horse may need more training before you can reasonably expect him to produce this in competition, especially with regard to his balance and outline and that, in the short term at least, you may need to ask for less length in competition than you can achieve at home so as to build up his confidence for the future.

'Onto shoulders'; 'should be more uphill'

Horses often push themselves onto the forehand in their early attempts at medium gaits, as they do not yet have the strength over their backs to lift their withers for more than a step or two in the bigger strides. By general training for more balance and self-carriage, this problem should start to resolve itself.

In competition:

- Take more care with your preparatory half-halts so that the horse starts the medium strides in his best balance.

- Be very conscientious about sitting tall, so that your weight stays away from his forehand.

- Whilst taking care not to disturb his rhythm, make small upward half-halts with your reins during the medium strides.

- Do not ask for more length than he can achieve without compromising his balance.

'Stiffened/came against hand in transition back'; 'lost/lacked balance in end transition'; 'quickened the steps during transition back'

Either you used too strong/abrupt rein aids, or your horse's training/strength is not yet sufficient for him to achieve this transition with ease.

You must pay great attention to developing correct downward transitions in training. A good exercise is to ride medium along the long side then at the end to turn him into shoulder-in (*push* his shoulders inward with a forward hand, don't pull your hands backward) and apply lots of leg; this will teach both of you to think *forward* into your downward transitions.

Quickening the steps during this transition is an avoidance of bringing the hind leg forward beneath the body and may be caused by strong rein aids or may develop as a poor habit if not noticed early on. If a horse does this habitually, you must hold your seat firmly to the correct rhythm of the gait during the transition and refuse to allow the quickened steps.

'Show transitions more clearly'

If a horse's training is correct and he can manage these transitions with relative ease, this is just a case of being a bit more demanding in the arena. Make sure that you are actually *asking* for clear transitions, and not just thinking about the medium without attention to the start and finish: many tests now have separate marks given for these transitions as a way of making riders focus more on their production.

In Medium/Lengthened Canter Strides

'Strides became quicker rather than longer'; 'speeded up'

Either you tried to produce medium canter with too much (or too quick) leg aiding, or he is running away from you. Either way, the answer is to have your controls more clearly *on your seat*. This involves insisting that he listens to the swing of your seat.

If he tends to run, you will need to use a degree of upper leg closure to hold the saddle to a slower speed, and so insist that he moves in harmony with you.

If you have been the cause, ensure that your legs are only truly active in the preparation phase, then swing your seat in the bigger sweep along the saddle *without* backing it up with your legs. You should be able to harness the impulsion you created in preparation to produce long, elastic strides without the excess leg that causes tension in the ribcage muscles and tightening of his frame.

'Haunches in'; 'leaning on outside shoulder'

'Haunches in' is a deliberate curling of the horse's body to the inside; a common problem associated with the asymmetrical sequence of legs at canter. This places his outside hind leg beneath his body, allowing him to avoid placing his inside hind directly beneath his body, i.e. engaging. This evasion is also often associated with stiffening of the back and/or hollowing, and pushing the croup up.

The horse that 'leans on his outside shoulder' is likewise avoiding engagement by allowing his weight to drop onto his shoulders which, combined with his psychological desire to lean towards the track for support, results in him carrying more weight on his outside foreleg.

The visible difference between these two faults is small and subtle, and although the latter is the easier of the two to correct, the mechanism of correction is the same for both.

- In the corner prior to the exercise (or on the track in the preceding 10 m or so), position the horse's shoulders more to the inside of the arena by bringing both hands slightly towards the inside of the arena, i.e. a *slight* shoulder-fore positioning, with minimal neck bend (see the diagram on page 195).

- As you ride the strides out longer encourage him to *slightly* lower and lengthen his neck position. This will prevent him from stiffening his back.

- Keep making small positioning aids to the inside to maintain his slight shoulder-fore position, as his body will keep trying to revert to the incorrect position that he favours. Carrying himself in this new alignment requires greater effort, which he will attempt to avoid until he becomes stronger.

- Practise this positioning diligently in training, as repetition of the exercise will not only form a new habit but will also develop the strength and flexibility in his inside hind leg to make this movement easier, so that he will no longer bother trying to avoid it.

'Changed lead'; 'went disunited'

There are several possibilities:

- You did not take enough care of your horse's straightness before asking for medium strides. (See above under correcting 'haunches in'.)

- Your seat slipped to the outside of the saddle. Some horses push their riders towards the outside; some riders lack established straightness in their position. Either way, such a shifting of weight may pull him off balance and cause/allow him to change leads either fully or partially. Have someone check while you are training that you are not slipping outward in this fashion.

■ He is changing behind (or fully changing lead) in an effort to avoid engagement of one hind leg. Horses naturally have one stronger and one weaker hind leg (natural crookedness). This is not necessarily a veterinary issue, although if this occurs frequently such a possibility should be investigated. Conformation may play a part, e.g. Arabian horses will often change behind as their long hind limbs with rather straight joints are hard to engage. Correcting this involves strengthening the weaker hind leg in training, and being very conscientious about maintaining your outside leg position (drawn back from the hip) to keep your weight in your inside seat bone.

■ You may have allowed your outside leg to slide forward (it should be maintained in an outside leg position at all times in canter), giving confusing messages to your horse, especially if he is more highly trained and understands flying changes. Pay attention to developing a clear difference between your inside and outside leg positions.

■ He may have lost balance, either to his forehand or towards one shoulder, and has changed as a result. Take care of your own upright posture to help him maintain balance and straightness.

'Downhill'; 'croup high'; 'pushing the croup up'

This is a balance issue that may or may not be deliberate.

■ If a horse has not yet learned to lower his croup (engage) in his general work, then this lack of balance must be expected. Use more transition work in training to improve both his engagement and his strength.

■ If he is naturally built croup high, there is not too much you can do about it, simply work on his ability to sit down as far as his conformation will allow.

■ If he deliberately pushes his croup up, he is attempting to dislodge you from the saddle and so reduce your seat/weight influence. You must sit right back down into your saddle (even if in the short term you need to lean back) and refuse to be budged. Use your weight in the back of the saddle to push his croup down – picture yourself sitting on his croup and *squash* it down!

22 Change of Leg through Trot

Examples of the change of leg through trot. (*Left*) HXF change the rein in working canter; between X and F change of leg through trot. (*Centre*) A half-circle right 20 m diameter; over X change of leg through trot; XC half-circle left 20 m diameter. (*Right*) FXH change rein in working canter; H change of leg through trot.

The change of leg through trot is performed either on a diagonal line or from one half 20 m circle to another and is distinct from the 'simple change' which requires walk steps between the two canters.

WHAT THE JUDGE WANTS TO SEE

* Clear and good quality canter on both leads.

* Around one horse's length (3–4 steps) of clear trot.

* Balanced and engaged transitions.

* No change in outline or suppleness over the back.

* The maintenance of correct alignment to the figure, both in terms of your horse's alignment (straightness) and the shape of the figure.

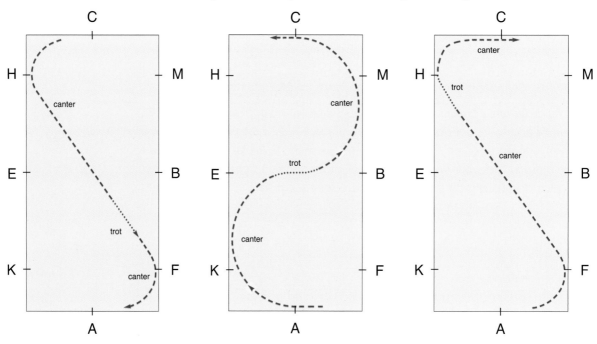

PREPARATION

Start preparing as always by achieving the best possible rhythm, balance and outline in your canter. As you approach your first transition, use small half-halts to take a little more weight back onto your horse's haunches. You should know by now how many strides before the transition you need to start asking.

On page 204, the left-hand diagram asks for the change to be performed between two markers, and you should aim to position your trot steps about halfway between them. The transitions in the centre diagram should be evenly spaced either side of X, *not* with the first transition *at* X; in the right-hand diagram – entering the corner – your downward transition should happen just before H and your upward transition as soon as possible, preferably as your body passes the H marker, because of the added complication of making a transition in a tight corner.

PRESENTATION

1. Try to keep your horse in a good balance in the downward transition.

2. Establish his trot rhythm immediately and clearly: do not rush this.

3. Changing, for example, from right to left lead: change your body from position right to position left and, as your hands both move to the left, move his shoulders from being *slightly* positioned and bent to the right, to *slightly* positioned and bent to the left.

4. Your weight should have moved slightly from your right seat bone to your left (though not enough to make him move sideways off your line) as you changed your body position. Now slide your right leg back and aid the left canter transition with your right leg and left seat bone.

5. Sit up tall and keep looking directly along the line of your figure.

TROUBLESHOOTING

'Fell onto forehand in downward transition'

Unless a horse's balance is simply not yet so good in downward transitions, you either left your preparatory half-halts too late, or you used too much strength in your rein aid.

Making the downward transition towards the end of a long straight line (see right-hand diagram) is tougher, as your horse has already had plenty of time to lose balance towards his shoulders before he gets anywhere near the transition. Spend more time working on his general balance, your aiding, and on his response to the half-halts; you will then have the tools to help him balance better in the first part of this movement.

'Hollowed'

■ Your horse may not yet be sufficiently secure in his outline in general.

■ You may have used too strong/abrupt a rein aid in the downward transition, causing him, justifiably, to hollow in protest.

■ He may have lost his balance onto his forehand in the downward transition (see above) and needed to raise his head to rebalance himself.

■ He may be anxious about the upward transition. Take time in practice to ride the first half of this movement *without* continuing into the second canter.

■ You may have alarmed him by rushing your aids; be calm and take your time through the transitions and the trot steps. It is better to have too many trot steps with a calm and round horse than to be precise on a stiff, tense and hollow horse.

'Hurried'

All the points listed under 'Hollowed' can also result in this movement being hurried, even if your horse does not lose his outline. Try to relax and take your time; insist that his trot steps are calm and rhythmic before going into the second canter, even if you have a few extra steps of trot.

If *you* are the anxious and speedy one, try to remember that you are there to *help* your partner and to make things as easy and comfortable as possible for *him*. With this in mind you should be able to be calmer and slower in your actions, and help him rather than fluster him.

'Crooked'; 'lost straightness'

■ If your horse fell onto his forehand during the downward transition, his haunches may well also swing to the side.

■ His natural crookedness is more likely to reassert itself under stress (such as competition), so take care to notice any crookedness, especially in the canter as you approach the transition and correct it by positioning his shoulders in front of his haunches.

- You may not have moved his shoulders from the old position (a slight shoulder-fore position towards the leading leg in canter) to the new position during the trot section, so that he was leaning onto one shoulder throughout the movement. Take care to move his shoulders from one position to the other, bearing in mind that he should always be functionally straight in canter (see the diagram on page 195).

'Wrong strike off'

You may have:

- Been unclear in your aiding/position/weight.

- Hurried your aiding, giving the horse insufficient time to respond.

- Failed to move his shoulders to the new direction.

So long as your training is sound, this mistake is almost always down to rider error, so take more time and care with your positioning and aiding.

23 Halts and Rein-back

Halts may be required in a number of places other than on the centre line, and for specified numbers of seconds.

Example
'C halt, immobility 4 seconds. Proceed in medium walk.'

Sometimes you will move forward out of the halt at walk or trot (and later in canter), and sometimes you will move almost directly into a rein-back.

Example
'A halt. Rein-back one horse's length (3-4 steps); proceed in medium walk.'

WHAT THE JUDGE WANTS TO SEE

Halts at Preliminary/Novice Level

- A smooth transition into a straight halt, which may be through a few steps of walk, with no resistance, stiffening or swinging.

- A continuously rounded outline, with your horse's attention on you, waiting for the signal to move off.

- Front feet square, with his hind feet not trailing. If one hind foot is further under the body than the other, this is acceptable at this level.

- Immobility for as long as the rider requires.

Halts at Elementary Level

- All the above features of the good halt, performed from a direct transition without any walk steps.

- The horse's hind feet must also be square and well engaged beneath his body.

Rein-back

- The rein-back starts from a clearly established, immobile halt.

- The backward steps are in clear diagonal pairs.

- The horse lifts his feet clearly off the ground and take fairly long but unhurried steps back.

- He remains in a round outline with no resistance in his mouth or stiffening of his body.

- He bends his hind leg joints and slightly lowers his croup, not dropping his poll and/or shoulders too low as he steps backward.

PREPARATION

Approach the halt from a rhythmic, active and balanced gait. From training you should know how soon you need to start asking him to halt. Remember that with a lazier horse you will need to use plenty of leg and little if any rein aid, as you want him to halt with his hind legs engaged underneath his body and *thinking* forward, even if you are going to ride rein-back. Even with the more forward horse use as little rein as possible, aiding the halt more by holding your seat and upper body still, with your legs drawn slightly back and closed onto his belly to draw the hind leg forward under him. If you absolutely have to use the rein, a light, vibrating contact may give you less stiffening and potential resistance than a resisting hand but, again, you should know from training the best way into a good halt for your individual.

PRESENTATION

Halt, Immobility

See Chapter 9 for the aids to the halt, and for maintaining immobility. Practise counting seconds – they are almost invariably longer than you think! One way to do it is to add in another word or two to your counting, e.g. 'one one thousand, two one thousand, three one thousand,' etc.; or 'one little second, two little seconds, three little seconds'. Try these out with a stopwatch and find what works for you. Far too many halts in tests are either too brief or too long. There are a number of other reasons your halt may not be of the correct length, but at least if you can count correctly you stand a better chance!

The first step of a rein-back, lifting the legs in clear diagonal pairing.

Rein-back

1. Take care to have a clearly established and immobile halt *before* asking for rein-back.

2. Take both legs slightly back and incline your upper body fractionally forward from the hips to lighten your seat.

3. Use small leg squeezes to ask for rein-back. Your rein contact should remain still so that the horse understands not to move forward, then should become very light as he steps back; *do not pull on the reins*, or keep a tight contact once he steps back as this will cause him to stiffen and/or resist.

4. Count the backward steps and as soon as you reach the required number/distance, sit upright and into your saddle, bring your legs forward into girth position and immediately apply them to ask him to move forward without halting.

TROUBLESHOOTING

Halts

'Resisted/hollowed into halt'

Unless you have a general problem with acceptance of the contact, you probably used too strong a rein aid, or else you failed to give your horse sufficient warning and applied your aids rather too late and as a consequence too strongly. When training, review the distance you need to bring him into halt without being too strong, and remember to plan ahead in your next test.

'Crooked halt'; 'swung haunches into halt'

See page 113.

'Halt not immobile'; 'fidgeting'

See page 114.

'Trailed hind legs in halt'

You need to use more leg and less hand during the transition to encourage your horse to step under his body with his hind legs. When working at home, help from the ground can assist him to form the habit of halting with his hind legs engaged (See Chapter 18 in *The Building Blocks of Training*, J.A. Allen.)

Rein-back

'Resisted'; 'hollowed in rein back'

Unless this is a training issue, you probably used too strong a rein aid or continued to keep too strong a contact once the rein-back began. If your horse fails to listen to you when you ask for rein-back, use a sharper *leg* aid to regain his attention, not a stronger contact.

If he tends to hollow during the rein-back, try to put his head and neck a little overdeep *before* you ask; this means that as he lifts his head during the rein-back he will only move it up *into* position, not above it.

'Steps back not diagonal'

There are a number of reasons why a horse's rein-back sequence might not be correct. The most likely are:

- His back hollowed.

- He hurried/was hurried back.

- He began from a disengaged halt.

- He is anxious about rein-back

- He lacks suppleness over his topline/in his hind leg joints.

Try to have him genuinely round and engaged in the halt prior to your rein-back, take care with your aids so that he doesn't feel pressurised, and regulate his steps back to a steady speed: you should be able to stop the rein-back on any step that you choose. Over time, with care, you should be able to recover the true diagonal sequence.

'Crooked rein-back'

The corrections for this problem are as for the crooked halt that always swings in one direction (see page 113). Also, practise rein-back in training either alongside a fence, keeping the fence always on the side towards which the horse swings, or between raised poles (make sure that they are safely supported and not so low that he will step over them) or hay/straw bales. Both of these exercises can help him to learn to step back straight.

'Ran back too fast'

You may have asked your horse to move too quickly; use your leg aids at the speed at which you want him to step: one aid to each step.

If he runs back of his own accord, practise rein-back by simply allowing him to move just one step back before asking him to go forward again. Once he takes that one step calmly, allow two steps back and repeat until he no longer rushes backward but waits for your aids, then build up to as many steps as you need.

'Reluctant'; 'dragging feet'

Make certain that you have an engaged and round halt: any hollowing of the horse's back will make rein-back uncomfortable and cause him to drag his feet. If he is slow to respond to your aids, use quicker, more insistent *leg* aids.

In training, ask him to rein-back more quickly than the speed he offers, possibly with help from the ground.

24 Leg-yield

Leg-yield is performed in trot, either a) from the centre line towards the track, or b) from the track to the centre line.

Examples

a) 'EA working trot; A down centre line; between D and L leg-yield left to S.'

b) 'K working trot; P-I leg-yield left; C track left.'

WHAT THE JUDGE WANTS TO SEE

- Consistent quality to the horse's trot in terms of rhythm, speed and suspension before, during and after the leg-yield.

- Continuously maintained outline and balance.

- No change in impulsion or suppleness over his back.

- The horse moving on a diagonal line with his body *nearly* parallel to the track, with his shoulders just *fractionally* in the lead.

- A slight flexion at the poll *away* from the direction in which he is travelling (you should just be able to see his nostril and eyebrow), but no bend through his body.

- His inside legs passing and crossing in front of his outside legs.

PREPARATION

1. Approach the leg-yield with your horse in the best rhythm and balance that you can achieve and if you are turning onto the centre line use the turn to help engage him.

2. If you are in rising trot, make a change of diagonal one stride before you begin your flexion change (see point 3 below); this will help to warn him of the approaching change of flexion as well as put you onto the correct diagonal for the movement.

3. A couple of steps before the leg-yield begins, ask for a slight flexion away from the direction in which you will be travelling. If, for example, you will be travelling towards the left, make a small vibration on your right rein and turn your shoulders fractionally to the right.

4. You need to bring your horse's shoulders *slightly* towards the intended direction of travel so that they can be just in advance of his haunches. Using the same left-travelling example, move both your hands (keeping them the normal distance apart) slightly to the left to move his shoulders, whilst still keeping the slight right position of your upper body.

(*Left*) Correctly positioned leg-yield to the left: Seven's shoulders are slightly in advance of his haunches and he has a small flexion at the poll to the right. His hind legs are clearly crossing. (*Right*) Leg-yield with shoulders too far in advance: 'falling out through the outside shoulder with too much neck bend'.

PRESENTATION

1. Start asking your horse to move sideways with your inside leg, i.e. inside relative to his flexion (in this left-travelling example, your right leg), *at* the girth. If you use it behind the girth you will push his haunches over faster and end up with them leading. Keep your outside leg back (outside leg position), but *off* him, or you may confuse him.

2. Use rhythmic on/off squeezes of your lower leg: try to time your leg closure to the moment his inside hind leg lifts into the air – this is the only moment in the stride when you can influence the leg to travel sideways and cross over in front of the other hind; you cannot affect the leg when it is the stance phase of the stride (on the ground).

3. As soon as he is moving sideways, return your hands to their normal position for a right flexion, with your outside rein against his neck to prevent him from falling through his outside shoulder, and your right rein maintaining flexion.

4. Your weight should be slightly more in your inside (right) seat bone and stirrup; if you either sit deliberately to the left, or you slip to the left, he will certainly move sideways, but he will be falling sideways to stay underneath you rather than carrying both of you sideways in balance.

5. When you near the track/centre line, *keep riding leg-yield*! Riders often give up a couple of steps short of completion and just drift forward rather than completing the movement by bringing the horse's haunches fully across until he is straight; this leaves the judge in no doubt about a rider's level of experience.

6. If you are in rising trot and your leg-yield finished at the track, you have no need to change diagonal at the end of the leg-yield, as you did that already at the beginning.

TROUBLESHOOTING

'Leaning on right/left shoulder', 'falling towards outside shoulder', 'trailing quarters', 'needs to be more parallel'

These comments all describe the same issue: the horse is losing his balance towards his leading shoulder and, as a consequence, that shoulder is too far in advance of his haunches (see photograph opposite).

■   Check your weight distribution: if you are sitting to the outside of the saddle, or with more weight in your outside seat bone, you will be pulling your horse off balance and towards that outside shoulder. This may also happen if you contract your inside leg upward in an effort to push him sideways, so lifting your inside seat bone. Try to deepen your inside leg position and heel, and drop your inside seat bone down. Alternatively think about lifting your outside seat bone up. Make a point of using your inside leg with a rhythmic squeezing, on and off, so that you alternately press your calf against his side then relax your leg and deepen your heel; this should prevent your leg from clutching upward and repeating the slide towards the outside.

■   Check your upper body position: are you turning from the waist *slightly* to the inside? Too much, and you may be causing your weight to slip to the outside.

■   Do you have your inside rein across his neck? You may find that you can push him sideways with an indirect rein, but it will also push him more out onto the outside shoulder – this is why it is called 'leg-yielding' and not 'rein-yielding'!

■ If the problem is that your horse has lost balance, your main task will be to prevent his shoulder from getting too far into the lead in the first place. This is the job of your outside contact: keep your elbow tight against your ribcage and your outside rein pressed against his neck (see the photograph on page 123).

'Not enough sideways'; 'failed to reach the marker'

To increase the angle at which you are travelling (i.e. to travel more directly sideways and less forward), coordinate a half-halt (squeeze of the fingers and tighter closure of the elbow) on your *outside* rein with the same moment that you use your *inside* leg. Do not:

■ Take your inside leg further back to push your horse over: you will only succeed in pushing his haunches into the lead.

■ Use your leg faster than the speed of his trot rhythm – this will cause him to speed up.

■ Shove harder with your leg – it is the coordination of leg and hand aid that you need; a harsher leg aid may result in him tightening his muscles against you and going even less sideways.

'Lost impulsion'; 'trot lost suspension'; 'steps too flat'

■ Try to keep his trot tempo up to speed; leg-yielding is hard work and he may slow down as a result, so use your leg at the speed that you want, not at the speed he offers you.

■ Make sure that in your efforts to ride sideways you are neither using so strong a rein contact that he cannot keep going, nor that you have stopped riding forward with your seat, i.e. kept your pelvis moving if you are in sitting trot.

'Haunches leading'

Check your aiding. It is possible that:

■ You did not position your horse's shoulders far enough into the lead before starting.

■ You drew your inside leg too far backward.

■ Your outside rein was so strong that you slowed his shoulders down too much.

25 Counter-canter

Counter-canter is introduced in tests in increasingly demanding patterns, starting with simple short straight sections of the track at Novice level, up to 20 m half-circles at Elementary level.

Examples

Novice level: 'FE change rein in working canter; ES counter-canter; S working trot.'

Elementary level: (In working canter left) 'FM one loop 5 m in from the track.' *and* 'VP half circle 20 m diameter in counter-canter.'

WHAT THE JUDGE WANTS TO SEE

- That the horse's quality of canter (speed, rhythm and 'jump') remains the same before, during and after the movement.

- That he does not attempt to change canter lead, or become disunited.

- That his outline does not change or stiffen.

- That he has a slight positioning towards his leading leg, but not an excessive bend.

- That he does not fall onto his forehand.

- That he keeps his hind legs engaged beneath himself, not trailing his hocks out behind.

- That he does not lean over (like a bicycle) to either side.

PREPARATION

Prepare your horse to produce his best possible engagement and balance: maintenance of counter-canter is only possible if his hind legs are underneath him to support his carriage.

PRESENTATION

Ride the required pattern with most of your focus on helping your horse to stay upright and balanced.

- Sit up, keep your seat firmly in the saddle and use it with a clear canter feeling (scooping downward and forward into the saddle at each stride so that you feel as if you are polishing the saddle from the back to the front).

- Keep *slightly* more weight in your inside seat bone and stirrup, where inside and outside are related to his *bend* and not to your direction of travel within the arena.

- Support him with a consistent rein contact, neither too tight nor too loose, and maintain a *slight* bend towards his leading leg.

- Keep your legs clearly in position: inside leg at the girth and outside leg drawn back (from the *hip*, not the knee – see the photograph on page 121).

Incorrect return to the track from a counter-canter loop. I have leaned to the left and used an over-strong indirect inside rein aid, causing poor Stanley to fall onto his outside shoulder with an excessive inside neck bend. He looks less than impressed!

To turn a horse in counter-canter:

1. Maintain your upper body, weight and leg positions in counter-canter as in true canter.

2. Without turning your shoulders from this position, move both of your hands towards his *outside* shoulder; your inside rein acts as an indirect rein, pushing his shoulders towards the other direction whilst still maintaining an inside bend, and your outside rein opens away from his neck to both lead and allow his shoulders to move towards the new direction.

3. Make sure to have a feeling of *pushing* forward with your hands, taking care not to pull them backwards towards your stomach.

4. Once you have him turned onto your line, bring your hands back into their normal position.

Moving the shoulders without changing the bend. Maggie is sitting clearly in position right but with both of her hands moved to the left. As soon as she has completed the turn she will replace her hands into their normal position. Use of this indirect rein is also appropriate when handling spooking inside the arena.

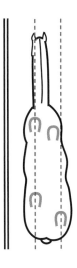

The relative position of the shoulders and haunches in left-lead counter-canter. The horse's two left hooves are on the same line with his nose directly in front of his left knee, i.e. not an excessive neck bend, and this line is parallel to the wall.

Throughout canter, both true and counter-canter, you should have your horse's shoulders slightly positioned towards the side of his leading leg (see page 195), so that if, for example, you are in counter-canter on the left lead, travelling around the arena clockwise, his shoulders should be slightly towards the left, i.e. closer to the arena boards than his haunches should be.

TROUBLESHOOTING

'Lost balance and broke'; 'became disunited'; 'changed leads'

If you receive these comments, ask yourself if your horse is sufficiently supple, balanced and engaged to accomplish counter-canter without difficulty? All of these physical skills need to have developed to some degree before you attempt counter-canter. If he stiffens, loses balance or if his hind legs do not keep jumping forward fast enough to stay underneath him, he will lose the gait.

Tension can also cause this problem by making him stiffen, as can a lack of confidence.

If he *is* capable, then you may have:

- Allowed him to drop onto his forehand, or you leaned forward, putting your body-weight over his shoulders.

- Not kept him sufficiently active.

- Lost your body, weight and/or leg positioning towards his leading leg.

- Had your rein contact too tight, blocking his hind legs.

- Ceased to swing your seat in a canter rhythm.

- Not maintained his body alignment with his shoulders slightly positioned towards his leading leg.

- Bent his neck too much with your inside rein, pushing him off balance onto his outside shoulder.

'Fell onto forehand'; 'trailing hind legs'; 'canter lost jump'; 'four-beat canter'

Many of the above problems also apply here: most of the problems that occur in counter-canter have the same causes and solutions. In particular, try to:
Sit up really tall and keep a firm upper body tone – think about having your weight nearer to your horse's haunches than to his shoulders.

- Support him with a firm but forward (and not too short) rein contact.

- Use *quick* leg aids to speed up his hind legs. Do not just try to be stronger with your legs as this will tend to push him forward more powerfully and he will find it hard to balance.

- Take care to move your seat clearly in a canter rhythm, but not to use *too big* an action or you will push him into making his strides too long for him to manage.

'Hollowed'; 'stiffened the back'

Do your best to keep your horse really round as you approach and move into the counter-canter, trying not to let him get above the bit: once you have lost the outline it will be very hard to regain it during the movement.

Take note of all the above advice on riding the counter-canter in general, as hollowness and stiffening are usually anxiety related, either due to lack of confidence about being able to stay in balance, or about the rider's ability to sit and aid the counter-canter without causing him problems!

'Leaning over'

This can be caused by stiffening (either as a result of anxiety or a general lack of suppleness), by the rider leaning to one side, or by a deliberate avoidance of the engaging effect of counter-canter.

Review the above corrections and hopefully you can eliminate anxiety.

If you are certain that your body position is not at fault, you may find that you are leaning to one side simply because your horse has leaned over and you have gone along with him. This may be habitual on his part, or it may be a deliberate attempt to avoid engagement. Either way, you must bring his body upright by sitting perpendicular *to the ground* and not to *him*! This might not be so comfortable for you in the short term, but neither is it comfortable for him, and he will adjust himself to your new position if you persist.

26 Simple Changes

A simple change is a change of canter lead through *walk*. Ideally the transitions involved should be direct, i.e. canter to walk and walk to canter, without any trot steps involved. In reality, at the earliest level at which this movement is required, a minimal number of trot steps are acceptable in the downward transition, but not in the upward.

WHAT THE JUDGE WANTS TO SEE

- A balanced canter in the approach.

- A direct (or almost so) transition from canter to walk, with the weight clearly taken back onto the haunches, not dropping onto the forehand or using a braced foreleg to arrest the momentum.

- Clear steps of relaxed walk showing a secure sequence for about one horse's length (approximately three steps).

- A direct transition from walk into the opposite canter lead.

- A consistent outline and soft acceptance of the contact throughout.

PREPARATION

At the early levels the pattern is designed to assist with your preparation: in both examples in the diagrams, there is a short turn (or half-circle) immediately before the downward transition which will make a degree of collection easier to achieve.

Don't just ride around the turn; *do* use half-halts as you ride the turn to help him to take weight back onto his haunches.

- Sit very tall and make small rhythmic squeezes on your inside rein, whilst using plenty of inside leg.

- Keep your seat action small so that you ask him to shorten his strides; with your supporting leg aids he should step his hind leg more under himself and so lighten his forehand.

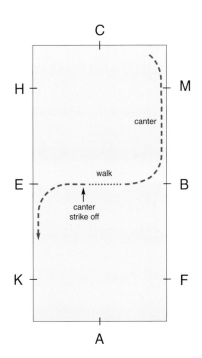

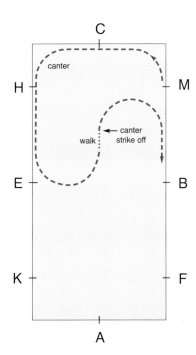

Two examples of a simple change. (*Left*) 'B turn right; X simple change of leg; E track left.' (*Right*) 'MH collected canter; between H and E half-circle left 10 m diameter to centre line, simple change and half-circle right 10 m diameter to between M and B.'

PRESENTATION

1. Aim to make your downward transition several metres *before* you arrive at the marker or the position where you are required to perform the simple change. **It is better to make the downward transition too early than too late.** For example, in the example shown in the right-hand diagram above you may make the downward transition *before* you have fully straightened him onto the centre line.

2. As soon as the horse breaks into walk, relax. A correct walk sequence is only possible when his long back muscles are relaxed; this also depends on him being in a round outline because any hollowness will stiffen and tense these critical back muscles.

3. During the walk steps, you must move his forehand from the old position (slight shoulder-fore position towards the side of the old leading leg), to the new side. In the example in the left-hand diagram above that is from position right to position left. If you fail to move his shoulders, he will strike off incorrectly, back onto the previous lead.

4. You should walk for three to four steps (about one horse's length) as you pass over the position specified on the test sheet for the simple change. Try to position the walk section equally on either side of this position.

5. As you complete the walk steps, ask for canter; your upward transition must be direct, any trot steps will lose marks.

6. Continue with the remainder of the required pattern.

TROUBLESHOOTING

'Fell onto forehand in downward transition'; 'downward transition too progressive'; 'too much trot down'; 'hollowed/against the hand to walk'

All of these comments indicate that your horse was not well enough prepared for the downward transition. Assuming that his training level is sufficient for him to be able to perform this movement, then you must take more care next time to *use* the turn/half-circle before the simple change to sit him down more onto his haunches in the manner described in the Preparation section above.

'No walk shown'; 'walk steps not clear'; 'not enough walk shown'; 'jogging'; 'poor sequence in walk'; 'tense over back'

The possible reasons for these comments are:

■ You may not have taken sufficient time to establish walk. Perhaps you were anxious because your downward transition was a little late, or you rushed the upward transition. Next time, take it more slowly. Prepare and maybe even make your downward transition earlier, then relax and insist on clear walk steps. Showing no walk steps at all can only ever gain an 'insufficient' mark: 4. Taking your time may make your upward transition late, or make the whole movement too protracted, but you will still have a better chance of gaining at least one more mark, and you set a better precedent for future tests.

■ Your horse became tense during the downward transition because you did not make sufficient preparation, or you were too abrupt/strong with your aids. Collection into a downward transition will only happen with co-ordinated, correct aids (see above under Preparation), never with over-strong hands.

■ Your horse anticipated the upward transition. This is more of a training issue and could take a while to solve. You need to practise the movement in training, but *without* performing the upward transition: just walk after the downward transition and remain in walk, possibly on a long rein, until he relaxes. You will need to repeat this procedure often for him to accept that a canter to walk is not *always* followed by a walk to canter.

'Wrong strike off'

This error is most likely down to the clarity of your aids – seat (weight), leg and rein – and your positioning of the horse's shoulders before asking for the strike-off onto the new lead. Take the time to get it right because this most often occurs when riders rush the movement.

Also make sure to aid him in the correct moment within the walk sequence for the appropriate lead, i.e. as his outside forefoot comes to the ground. You will see his outside shoulder moving back towards you; this is the only moment in the walk sequence when he can change to the correct canter sequence.

'Upward transition not direct'; 'should be more direct to canter'; 'lazy to canter'

Again, this is likely to be a training issue; does he genuinely listen to your legs? Or it may be due to a lack of clarity in your aiding.

- Did you take your new outside leg back clearly, from the *hip*, not just from the knee?

- Did you have your weight into your inside seat bone, and did you *use* that seat bone with a push forward along the saddle to aid the strike-off?

- Did you aid him in the correct moment within the walk sequence (see section above)? If you did not coordinate your aids correctly then he may have delayed or had a muddled response due to confusion.

- For more details on transition aiding, see Chapter 17 in *The Building Blocks of Training* (J.A. Allen)

'Tense/hollow transitions'; 'lost/lacked straightness'

Whilst at first glance these might seem to be unrelated issues, both problems are in fact the result of loss of balance and of tension. In both cases you must take more care with your preparation for the downward transition to enable your horse to remain round and balanced and, as a result, straight.

They may also both be the result of too strong or rigid a use of the reins. Try to keep your contact more relaxed, and not to draw your hand backward, i.e. learn more about using your seat and body to perform downward transitions rather than relying on your hands.

27 Half Walk Pirouettes

Example
'K collected walk and before V large half walk pirouette right, proceed in collected trot'

A half walk pirouette is a demanding and complicated exercise. Before you even attempt one you should be able to coordinate your legs with the lifting of his hind legs – touching him with your right leg as his right hind lifts into the air and vice versa – and to *slightly* collect his walk (i.e. slightly reduce the ground cover of his steps) without him becoming tense, resistant or losing impulsion. He must also be responsive to moving his haunches away from your outside leg aids.

WHAT THE JUDGE WANTS TO SEE

- That the horse maintains the quality (sequence) of his walk throughout the movement.

- That he remains supple over his back and soft in your hands, with a continuously rounded top line.

- That he maintains his impulsion, lifting both hind legs equally throughout.

- That his front end moves around his haunches whilst his hind legs mark time. For a *large* half walk pirouette his hind feet should make a half circle of around 3 m diameter.

- That he maintains an inside bend.

- That he keeps his weight back on his haunches.

- That he moves out of the pirouette with activity and in a good carriage.

- For a *large* half walk pirouette, when he will finish the half turn on an inside track, a return to the track *on a straight line*, and not by moving laterally (in half-pass).

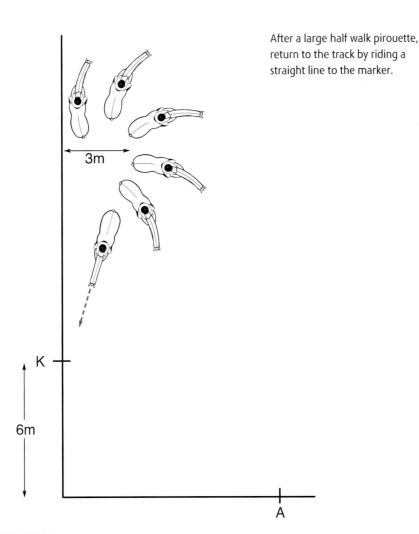

After a large half walk pirouette, return to the track by riding a straight line to the marker.

3m

K

6m

A

PREPARATION

1. Collect the walk a little; the horse must keep accepting your hands and stay supple over his round top line as you ask him to shorten his steps without losing activity. Take care not to be strong with your hands but use frequent small half-halts.

2. Put him into a *slight* shoulder-fore position: for right pirouette bring his shoulders very slightly to the right, but also have your outside leg back to start exerting control over his haunches, i.e. don't let them swing out.

PRESENTATION

1. Bring your weight clearly over onto your inside seat bone – in this example, the right.

2. Turn your upper body to the right and with a *very* light contact start to *push* the horse's shoulders round by pressing your outside rein against his neck (see the photograph on page 123) whilst your inside hand leads him round by being slightly opened away from his neck. Whatever you do, *do not pull backward or be rigid in your hands/forearms*: there should be *almost* no weight in your contact.

3. While pushing the shoulders round, simultaneously close your outside leg (in outside leg position) against his belly.

4. Throughout the movement, use your legs in an alternating walk rhythm – left, right, left, right – with your legs coordinated to his hind legs. If you feel him try to swing his quarters out, use your outside leg more strongly; if he tries to lose impulsion use your inside leg with more strength, but always *maintain this rhythm.*

5. Finish the half-pirouette by straightening onto a line that leads directly back towards the track (see diagram on page 227).

TROUBLESHOOTING

'Resisting'; 'hollow'; 'stiffened'

If you receive these comments, you were almost certainly using too strong or too rigid a rein contact.

Although you need to collect the horse's walk in the approach, this should be done with small half-halts, remembering to *release* your contact after every stronger moment. During the half-pirouette itself, you should feel as if you have *next to no contact* at all, *pushing* his shoulders round with a really forward feel to your hands.

If you prepared him successfully (by moving weight back onto his haunches and finding smaller but still active steps) you should be able to hold him in the pirouette with your body position and between your two legs; you should not need to use your reins to prevent him from stepping forward out of the pirouette but just for turning his forehand.

'Lost impulsion'; 'stuck'; 'needs more activity'

You either used too much rein or insufficient leg aids. The former would cause the horse's back to stiffen and block his inside hind leg from stepping forward, which is particularly likely if you used a strong *inside* rein. (See the previous section for more details on how to use your hands correctly.)

If your leg aids were insufficient, they were either not strong enough or not in the correct timing. Review the timing of your leg aids in walk and make a clear effort to keep this going during the pirouette. If your timing is fine, then use a stronger leg aid but still maintaining the rhythm. Of course the horse must also be responsive to your leg!

It is also possible that you were overambitious with the size of your pirouette, asking for a smaller diameter than he is yet able to manage. If this is the case, next time ride the figure a touch bigger, feeling as if you are riding him a little more *forward* in each step.

'Lost quarters'; 'haunches swung out'; 'pivoting'

You may have caused this problem by using too strong a rein so that your horse was physically unable to step his hind leg forward underneath himself (see previous section).

Alternatively, you may have simply lost control of his haunches.

- He must respond correctly to your displacing leg, i.e. when you close your outside leg he must move away from it.

- You must make sure you take your outside leg far enough back, and to use it in the correct timing – as his outside hind lifts into the air. Using your leg when his hoof is on the ground is wasted effort; you can only displace the hind leg when it is in the air.

- Check that your weight does not slip to the outside: he will swing his haunches outward to stay beneath your weight. He may also *push* you to the outside of the saddle – keep moving yourself back to the inside every time this happens, even if you feel like you are hanging off the saddle to the inside!

'Needed more bend'; 'wrong bend'

You may have forgotten to ask for sufficient inside bend: you should be able to see the rear corner of your horse's inside eye during the whole movement. If you prepare using shoulder-fore, you should already have an inside flexion, and as you lead him around with your inside hand (in an open-rein position) and your upper body turned to the inside, he should maintain this position.

Another possibility is that you were too strong with your *outside* rein in your efforts to turn him, and you *disallowed* the bend. Your outside hand should have an *inward and forward* feel in the direction of his inside ear so that your outside rein presses against his neck but with little weight in your hand.

Less likely, but still possible, is that your weight shifted to the outside of the saddle (see previous section) and your outside seat bone pushed into the saddle rather than your inside seat bone; this would suggest to your horse to bend in the opposite direction.

'Thinking backward'; 'stepped back'

This problem could be the result of too much rein, not enough leg, or your horse dropped behind your aids. Whatever the reason, the solution is the same: lighten your contact extremely, use strong leg aids and ride the figure more forward, i.e. *bigger*.

'Big'; 'too large'; 'too much sideways'

You may be riding the figure deliberately larger for one of the reasons already covered, and if this is the case you must simply put up with these comments in the knowledge that with more training you will be able to reduce the size later.

If this is not the case, it may be that you are not asking him to turn his shoulders quickly enough; this will also produce the 'too much sideways' comment, as he appears to half-pass around a small circle. You must try to turn his shoulders more quickly than his haunches. Think of his body as being like one hand of a clock: the pointer end moves much faster than the end near the centre of the dial. Try to move his front end round like the pointer end of the clock hand, i.e. much faster than his haunches but, as you do this, just take care not to hurry the whole thing too much or you may cause other problems!

28 The Final Centre Line

Do not ignore the end of your test. Many riders feel that they have finished the test when they complete the last movement and do not ride a good finish, losing unnecessary marks.

Take as much care with your final centre line as you did with your entry: it is your last chance to leave the judge with a good impression in their mind as they settle down to write those final 'collective' marks while you are leaving the arena.

WHAT THE JUDGE WANTS TO SEE

- A well-balanced turn onto the centre line, with clear inside bend.

- A well maintained outline, rhythm and straightness as you proceed towards the halt, including during any transitions that are required on the centre line.

- An immobile, straight halt.

- A correct salute.

Maggie and Seven leave the arena at free walk, pleased with how their test has gone.

After this, the judging ceases, and so you can praise your horse as you like whilst you leave the arena – the judge will already be writing up the end comments – but make sure that you remember to make that final salute *before* you praise your horse or exit the halt.

Examples
'A down the centre line; G halt, immobility, salute.' Also: 'X halt.' and 'Between X and G halt.'

This is the most basic end to a test, and all the components have been covered previously: treat the turn at A as if it is a half 10 m circle and straighten immediately onto your centre line.

Example
'A down centre line; X medium walk; G halt, immobility, salute.'

Remember to ride *forward* in your downward transition to walk, making sufficient preparation before you arrive at X and with as little rein aid as possible – this will help to reduce any resistance or hollowing to a minimum and keep him straight.

Ride the walk actively forward, but do not aid it too strongly or you may cause him to jog or resist; at this point err on the side of caution.

Riding halt out of walk also needs preparation or he may either resist the contact or swing his haunches. Approaching the halt from trot is often easier than it is from walk, as the extra impulsion assists in maintaining straightness, so do not automatically assume that halting from the walk is going to be easy.

Example
'EX half circle 10m diameter; G halt, immobility, salute.'

Take care to finish your half-circle clearly *on* the centre line; if you overshoot, it will be very hard to straighten, as you do not have far to go before the halt. This movement must be clearly and distinctly a half-circle of the right depth, as opposed to the movement: 'E turn left; X turn left; G halt, immobility, salute', which should show clear and distinct turns, with just a step or two on the half school (E–B) line, and not beyond.

Example
'A down centre line; D collected trot; LX (G) medium trot; just before G progressive transition; G halt, immobility, salute.'

This ending starts to prepare you for more advanced tests where you may be asked to do other things on the final centre line in addition to halting. Bear in mind that the judge sitting at C cannot easily estimate the *size* of the strides from head on, but can clearly see the rhythm and tempo, and the balance. Do not ride such an enthusiastic medium trot that you drive your horse onto his forehand and fall into a heap at G. Clearly you need to show some difference, but unless you have more than one judge (as you will do in championship classes) then, again, err on the side of a more conservative size of stride to make your halt easier.

If your horse can manage a really big medium trot and remain balanced, then go for it!

29 Freestyle Tests

Test Construction

There are many different ways to construct a freestyle test: you may have a piece of music that you want to interpret, you may start with a floor plan and have music fitted later, you may do your own music with a music software editing package, or you may pay a professional company or individual to do it for you.

The possibilities and combinations are quite extensive and it is up to you to decide which way you want to go about it. There are also many articles and in-depth books written on the subject if you feel that you want more help. The purpose of this chapter is to give you an insight into the construction of an interesting test that will show off your horse's good points and minimize the impact of his weaker work, and to guide you through the procedure on the day of competition.

The Floor Plan

At each test level there is a Freestyle test sheet detailing the compulsory movements that you *must* show during your test. You can also include any other movements that you choose that are in other tests *at that level*; you must *not* show movements from a higher level or you will be given penalty points. Including other movements can enhance your choreography mark, but you will only get marked directly for the compulsory movements.

If you choose to show a movement more than once, you will be given a mark on your sheet for each time you perform it, with an average mark given as the final score.

These test sheets also tell you how long your test must be, e.g.: 'Minimum 4½ minutes, maximum 5 minutes'.

What are Your Horse's Strongest Points?

- Start by deciding where you are going to halt. So long as you enter from A and halt facing the judge on the centre line, the actual location of the halt is your choice. You can also choose the gait at which you enter to give yourself the best halt, although entering at walk is less than impressive. You might choose to halt within the first few metres, or you may halt nearly at the end of the centre line: the allowed time for the test starts from your *move off from the halt* and not from your entry. Your choice of where you halt will affect the way your test begins: in freestyle tests it is better to turn away from the centre line in a half-circle or onto a diagonal line, rather than just go straight on down it as you do in a conventional test, because this adds interest. Take care to both enter and leave the halt with transitions that are permitted at your chosen level, e.g. *not* going from halt directly into canter in a Novice test.

- Pick your horse's best gait and start your test with it. There is no requirement to ride the test in the order that most tests are constructed – trot, walk, and then canter – the choice is entirely yours. You want to make a big impression on your audience, particularly the judge, so start with your most impressive gait. If this happens to be the walk – then go for it!

- From the test sheet, pick out the movements that you think your horse is best at: it may be circles; it may be certain transitions or movements. Start with these highlights in mind and place them most prominently in your test, i.e. perform them close to the judge and where she can best see them. For example, if your horse does a good trot to canter transition, put it right over the centre line in the top half of the school where the judge has an excellent view of it, *don't* hide it in the furthest corner at the A end of the school, or on a straight line towards the judge where she cannot appreciate how nicely engaged your horse is.

- Start to build your pattern around these strong points, with a big start and then spread your weaker work through the latter half of the test; by then you will have impressed the judge with your best work and although she will notice your weaker work it will not be foremost in her mind.

What are Your Horse's Weakest Points?

- Your horse might, for example, have a poor walk sequence: in this case ride your walk straight toward the judge where she cannot see the sequence of his footfalls. Alternatively, use a pattern such as a small circle that can help to improve his sequence by relaxing his back, and position it at the farthest end of the arena from the judge.

- If he tends to throw his head up in trot/canter transitions, try positioning them so that you are riding directly away from the judge: your own body will obscure the judge's view!

- If his simple changes are difficult, place them where he is most likely to find them easiest – probably off a small half-circle.

- If medium trot is tough, don't ask him for too much; there is no requirement for this to be ridden on a full length diagonal, use a short diagonal or, better yet, put it on a long side where he can gain psychological support from the track. Don't repeat it unless you think the second performance will be better: you only *have* to show it once.

Of course these 'tricks of the trade' will not be so helpful when you ride in a championship class with more than one judge sitting in positions other than at C, but the principles still hold – and you have to get to that championship first!

Riding in a freestyle championship: the author competing on Welsh Cob, Pentrefelin Cymraeg, in the Novice Freestyle Championship class at the British Dressage Winter Championships.
Photograph by Image Point Event Photography

Adding Interest

- Try to find new and interesting positions within the arena to place your movements. Try not to put them in places where they occur in standard tests. Clearly you don't have this option with some patterns – it's very hard to make a 20 m circle interesting – but wherever possible use unusual parts of the arena, e.g. quarter lines and inner tracks; start movements between markers and link them together in unusual ways; ride a diagonal from the centre line at A to the track at H.

- Ride transitions that are not expected, such as riding directly into counter-canter, or make a simple change from true canter into counter-canter.

- Start a recognised movement, such as a serpentine, and partway through it, change it into something else, like a circle, or incorporate 15 m circles into the peaks of the serpentine loops (see the diagram on page 183).

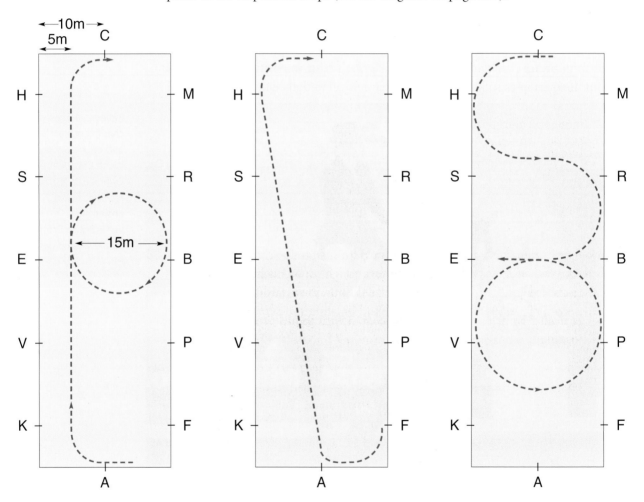

Unusual patterns that could be used in a freestyle test. (*Left*) Ride along a quarter line and then ride a 15 m circle before returning to, and continuing along, the same quarter line. (*Centre*) A diagonal line from A to H. (*Right*) Ride two loops of a serpentine and then a 20 m circle.

- Construct your programme with a degree of flexibility, particularly in the positioning of gait changes. Different arenas ride at surprisingly different speeds (owing to different arena surfaces and construction) and you will find that you do not always arrive at the same place in terms of both position and music each time you ride your test. You can always put in a circle if you are really far ahead of your music, but this is rather obvious padding and a flexible programme – say with a loop that can be ridden to a different depth to either absorb music or catch up with it – will be less obvious.

The Finish

- Try constructing a test that leaves open the exact place where you will turn onto the centre line. If you know your music well you should be able to arrive at your halt on the final beats, not get there so early that you have to sit and wait for the music to finish.

- Go for a big finish *if you can*. Medium trot down the centre line is always spectacular – so long as you don't fall in a heap as you try to halt! Walking into your final halt is a bit of a damp squib, even if your last work is in the walk.

There are always likely to be some compromises when you construct a test for individual horses: despite my advice that you don't enter in walk because this does not make a big opening impact, for some this might be the best option to get a good first halt. You should know your horse well enough to construct the test to showcase his best work.

The Music

Music is a very individual choice. Make sure to pick something that you really *like* – you will be listening to it a lot!

Choose your music

- The type of music that you decide to use will depend on personal choice but, unless you have the money to have a piece specially constructed for you, the best music to use is something that is recognisable such as film/TV themes, pop music, well-known classics, or jazz. *You* might prefer something a bit unusual, but unless it is really catchy when first listened to, it probably won't do it for your audience, and that includes the judge! Try *not* to pick something that was used a lot by other competitors the previous year – judges get very bored with the same music when they hear it four or five times in one class.

- You will need at least three pieces – one for each gait, chosen to match each of his three gaits in terms of tempo. You may do this technically, using a metronome or counting his beats per minute, or if you have a musical ear you may just hear pieces that you think will fit and try riding to them. Technology these days means that, within reason, you can change the tempo of a piece to suit your needs.

- You may decide to use a piece of music for the entry that is not one of those you have chosen to represent the gaits during the test – perhaps a fanfare – but try not to use too many different pieces or it will make the test rather bitty.

- Whatever you choose, you need some coherence between the pieces: they all need to be of the same type. For example, don't mix jazz and classical, or pop and theme.

- The *type* of music needs to be suitable to the type of horse: e.g. light classical for a Thoroughbred, strong heavy beat for a Cob, powerful music for a powerful horse.

- Vocals are rarely well received. From the judges point of view they are distracting and if you decide to use them, try to pick only vocals that are not too strident.

- Actually *finding* suitable music is often the longest process. Unless you listen to a wide variety, you may find that the easiest route is to buy one of the many CDs that are professionally produced especially for riding. The downside to this is that you are more likely to find other people using the same music as you.

Putting together a soundtrack

You have two options: have a soundtrack done professionally or do it yourself. The first can be expensive but there are many companies offering this service, some of them quite reasonable. This is clearly the least time consuming and the easiest, but is not to everybody's taste.

If you choose to put your own soundtrack together, probably using one of the many music editing software packages available, there are a number of important rules to follow.

- Entry music (not essential, but it does make a good impression) should crescendo at the halt. Check how long a piece of entry music is permissible – rules do change, and may vary between governing bodies.

- Having a brief silence for the entry halt is best if the move off is to different music.

- *Never* make a musical change mid-phrase – always finish and start pieces at the end or beginning of a full phrase.

- Using a slight fade out and fade in can make the join between two pieces less of a jar, but avoid a silent gap between pieces.

- Try to finish on a crescendo – the final halt should be triumphant, not a fade out or a vague ending. You might have to spend ages listening to the end of your chosen piece and timing how long that chunk of music is from the start of a whole phrase to the end of the piece to get it to fit with your proposed programme, but it will be worth it.

- If you are burning your CD on a computer, use only *writable* CDs; rewritable CDs will only play on a computer, *not* on a sound system.

Music licence forms

Once you have your music ready you must complete the licence forms that you can obtain from British Dressage. The sub-licence simply needs signing. For the record form you must state:

1. The name of the artist.

2. The title of the track.

3. The length of the piece of track that you have used.

British Dressage will also have sent you some labels to stick onto your CD case, one of which requires you to enter the above information so that it is visible.

Know your music

Before you ever get anywhere near to a competition arena you should know your music so well that you can mentally place at any given bar of the music exactly where you should be in your test pattern.

As already mentioned, different arenas ride at different speeds and you will need to adjust the way you ride the pattern so that you always end up in the right position for each critical change of gait, and for that impressive ending you have planned. This might involve cutting corners or going deeper into them, or making serpentine loops or half circles bigger or smaller. Remember: *the judge does not know your test!* She will have no idea what you planned, or if you are changing it as you ride. As long as you show all the required movements and the whole thing looks smooth and fits the music, that is all that the judge needs to be able to mark your test.

On the day

- Always have *two* copies of your music with you. The format may have been dictated in the schedule; CDs are usual, but check when you enter the class. As above, ensure that you have the right type of CD, and it can even be advisable to make your two copies on different computers – sound systems can be amazingly temperamental.

- Hand in your CDs when you arrive at the show. Make sure that they are fully labelled (see above), and also show your own name, your horse's name, your class, number and riding time for this show.

- Also put on instructions about your start, e.g. 'Start when I raise my hand by E', and any other information, e.g. 'Not too loud, please'!

- Once the bell has rung for you to start, take yourself to your chosen start point and raise one hand to indicate for your music to begin. You may want to stand still until your music starts, or you may keep moving – the choice is yours.

- *Listen* to your music as you ride, and ride to it. *Do not* just ride your pattern as you may not have his steps in synchronisation with the beat, or your changes of gait with the musical transitions, and this will drastically affect the whole appearance of the programme.

- After your ride is over, remember to collect your CDs!

30 After the Class

After-class Checklist

Collect your Score Sheets

Studying your score sheets is an important part of competing as they give you impartial feedback on areas of your training that need attention. *Don't forget to collect them!*

Even if you were not happy with your performance, or with the marks that you were awarded, you should still read your sheets: they may give you a different perspective on your weaker points and help you to improve your score at your next competition.

You will not be able to collect your sheets until after the whole class is completed, just in case there are any queries about individual scores. On the odd occasion that the same judge is judging two consecutive classes in which you are competing, you will not be able to collect any sheets until after *both* classes are completed.

If you don't want to wait until a class is finished, organisers are usually quite willing to send your sheets to you by post (as long as you leave payment and address/SAE). Don't forget to arrange this with the secretary – they will not do it unless requested to.

The Prize-giving

If you are fortunate enough to be required for a prize-giving, you *must* attend it to be eligible for any prizes. Organisers/sponsors are well within their rights to withhold any prizes if you fail to present yourself for a prize-giving. Often, this is the only time a sponsor will come face to face with competitors, and it is an opportunity for them to get something back from the money that they have donated in terms of publicity (photographs and write-ups in the press) and personal contact with potential customers.

You should check with the secretary regarding the time and location of a prize-giving, and if you are required to be mounted or on foot. Even unmounted you should present yourself in smart attire, preferably in full competition clothing. Mounted prize givings can range from the full line-up (as many as ten competitors) mounted, to just the top one, two or three mounted with the remainder on foot. If you have a horse who is nervous or dangerous in a prize-giving, you can ride a substitute, or if necessary have a groom with a lead rein; in extreme cases, ask the organiser if you can be excused from being mounted, but you should only do this if you truly have safety concerns for yourself or those around you.

Stabling

If you have stabled your horse at the show make sure before you leave that the stable and surrounding area are clean and tidy, and don't forget to check that you have collected all your gear.

Saying 'Thank You'

If a class is sponsored, it is always good to write a note of thanks to the sponsor because, if the sport of competitive dressage is to prosper, and for competitions to be able to offer prizes or prize money, having a sponsor is often a requirement not a luxury. Riders should therefore, if they wish to continue competing, always try to acknowledge sponsors or they may choose not to continue with sponsorship in future years.

Similarly, organisers deserve a 'thank you', whether verbal or written. Unless you have organised a dressage competition yourself, you probably have little idea of the amount of work needed behind the scenes before the competition day, not to mention the clearing up afterwards!

Many organisers, secretaries and officials give their time free for the love of the sport, and receiving a 'thank you' can make all the difference. After all, if these people did not put in the effort, there would be no shows for you to compete in, and so a 'thank you' may make all the difference to whether a show continues to be held or not.

Speaking to the Judge

Most judges will be quite willing to discuss and elaborate upon the comments that they have put on your sheets if you approach them after a class. Ask politely first if they are willing to do so because it is their choice; there will be occasions when they do not have the time and, remember, judges are not required to talk to you.

Neither are judges obliged to justify their comments, and so if you have strong negative feelings after a class, do not approach the judge. Go home and cool down, and then start thinking about your sheets calmly: judges *do not* set out to be negative about a competitor's performance; they can only comment on what they see before them on the day, so you should try to understand what it was in your performance that led them to make their observations.

Unless you know the judge personally, avoid telephoning them at home to discuss things unless perhaps you also want to arrange some coaching with them, if this is something that they do.

Electrolytes

Finally, don't forget that if your horse sweated at the show he should have electrolytes put in his feed that evening. These essential salts cannot be built up or stored within the body and so whenever he sweats he will need to have them replaced.

31 Understanding Your Score Sheet

The Judge's Job

Gaining positive feedback from your test sheet is easier when you have a clear understanding of what the judge's job actually *is*! (For ease, I have called the judge 'she' throughout this book, and apologise to all male judges.)

As well as giving fair marks for the work that she sees *on the day*, the judge's remit is to set standards, and to help riders and trainers by **observing and making appropriate comments**. The remit is *not* to:

- Make training suggestions.

- Criticise you because she 'doesn't like' the breed/size/colour of your horse.

- Place those she knows/trains/likes/is in awe of, because they are 'big names'.

All of these, and other very similar, comments can be heard around the scoreboards or after the sheets have been released, and to a very large extent such personal reactions are due to a misunderstanding of the judge's job and the limits within which a judge must work. Let me elaborate on the above points.

A judge is required to make observations, not make training suggestions. Take, for example, a horse that is above the bit; the judge's observation would be along the lines of: 'above bit', 'should be rounder', 'not working through the back'. She will try to phrase it in such a way as to help you understand what the root of the problem is, e.g. not accepting the contact, stiff over the back etc., but what she is *not* there to do is to say: 'why don't you try a, b or c to get him to come into a rounder outline'. Another example is the horse who picks up the wrong canter lead. In this case the observation might be: 'wrong lead' or 'wrong strike-off', *not*: 'try doing this with your outside leg and that with your inside hand to achieve a correct strike-off'.

'Wrong lead', might sound like a blindingly obvious comment to you, but *that is the judge's job*. It is up to *you* to go away and find out how to put this problem to rights, either by taking more care to establish this piece of training at home before you compete again, or by discussing it with your trainer so that *they* can suggest how to put it right.

'This judge doesn't like my horse/has never liked my horse.' This is a very frustrating comment for a judge to overhear. Judges do *not* take a dislike to individual competitors or their mounts; what they fail to be impressed by is the *training* that they are being shown. If a judge gives you poor marks every time they see you, try to take on board their comments and do something about that aspect of your training. It is no good going out to compete week in week out, trying to find a different judge who *might* like your horse; whilst you are doing this, you are not sorting out the training issues that need to be dealt with at home.

Whilst some people are convinced that certain judges 'don't like' some breeds or types, particularly Arabian horses or cob types, or even small ponies, it is *not* the individual (or even the type) that they are marking down, it is the *way of going*. There is no question that certain types find the demands of dressage more difficult than others: Arabs tend to have long hind legs with high (and often weak) hocks which are hard to engage and the croup will often still be high even when the horse is making an effort, simply owing to conformation. On the contrary, there have been some Arabs, with more appropriate conformation, who have competed successfully at Advanced level.

Cob types tend to be upright in the shoulder and find medium gaits hard, or impossible, to produce – again, an effect of conformation – yet they are often strong behind and collect easily and can be seen doing well up to Medium level.

Ponies may have the 'daisy-cutting' action preferred in the show ring, but not the rounded action desired for dressage. On the other hand, more warmblood-type ponies are around nowadays and competing very successfully against the bigger horses.

To summarise, judges do not *dislike* certain combinations: they simply observe and comment on the way of going, measuring that way of going against their mental template of the way of going of the 'ideal' horse.

Judges should not be influenced by the rider in front of them. The judge's job is to mark every movement individually as it is performed on the day, without reference to how that combination has performed in the past, and without taking notice of who is in the saddle. The rules state that judges should not (except in exceptional circumstances, e.g. if asked to stand in for another judge at the last minute) judge anyone they train on a regular basis. They should likewise not be influenced by 'names', but you need to take into account that those people *became* 'names' because of their proficiency at competing. Even when they ride difficult horses it is likely they will still do a good job and probably gain a higher mark than someone of less experience would be able to produce from the same horse.

Affiliated judges undergo rigorous training and examinations before they are listed, and must attend compulsory ongoing training each year. This means that the standard of these approved judges will be fairly consistent, always allowing for the fact that they are still individuals and also human!

What the Marks Mean

The following marks are actually printed at the top of your score sheets.

10 – excellent
9 – very good
8 – good
7 – fairly good
6 – satisfactory
5 – sufficient
4 – insufficient
3 – fairly bad
2 – bad
1 – very bad
0 – not performed

When you collect your sheets, take notice of the mark for each movement, this will tell you exactly what the judge felt about each one even without the comments, which are an explanation of *why* she felt that way. Remember that she is judging each movement separately, not an overall picture of the whole test.

Judges should always give an explanatory comment when giving a mark of 5 or less, but will often not make comments when giving the higher marks, allowing these to speak for themselves – writers/scribes/secretaries have enough to write down as it is! For much the same reason, there will be a minimal number of positive comments on your sheet, not because the judge hasn't seen positive things in your presentation, but simply because there is relatively little time when judging to say too much. If you are in doubt about this, or would like to see things from the judge's point of view (an excellent way of learning), contact an organiser and find out who is judging at the next show. Telephone the judge and ask if you may sit in with her: most judges are only too willing to allow this, but some are not, and not under all circumstances, so be polite and understanding if they decline, and then try another judge instead.

The Scales of Training

The scales of training are the foundation for both training and judging. The judge will look to see that each scale is in place, going through the list in order until she

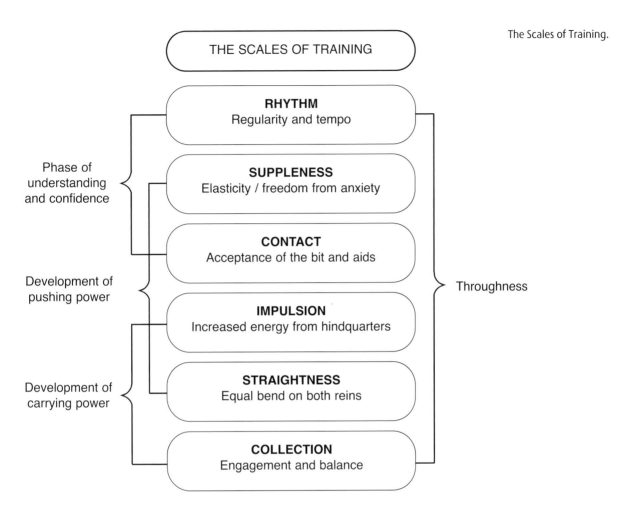

The Scales of Training.

finds one that is not fully accomplished. For example, when judging a change of rein at trot through two 10 m half-circles (see Chapter 14) in an Elementary-level test, she will check that your horse is showing and doing the following.

1. Relaxed and working in a good rhythm and tempo.

2. Showing suppleness and elasticity in both the body and the hind leg action.

3. Accepting the contact and your aids with confidence.

4. Moving with impulsion, i.e. controlled activity and engagement.

5. Equal bend to both sides.

6. A degree of collection that allows him to perform the whole movement with ease and precision.

This is slightly simplistic, but is designed to show how the judge orders her thoughts: if the first scale (relaxation and rhythm) is lacking, that will be the basis for her comment. If that scale is accomplished but your horse could be more supple, then that will be the main thrust of the comment, and so on. In other words, she will try to highlight for you the scale on which you should be concentrating in your training, as each scale is progressive, and although you cannot work on them in isolation from each other, you should be aware of the order of priority of each, i.e. there is no point focussing on impulsion (4) if you haven't got a decent contact (3), or on collection (6) if you don't have a straight horse (5).

Of course, judges are always learning too, and the more experienced the judge is, the clearer your sheet is likely to be!

The Collective Marks

These are the marks given at the end of your score sheet, written after you have exited the arena. They are designed to give an overview of your performance, with the marks reflecting those that you achieved during the test and the comments (and underlining of individual components of the collective marks) being a summary of your stronger and weaker points.

The first two – paces and impulsion – summarise the quality of your horse; the submission and the rider marks summarise the rideability of your horse, the correctness of the way you produced your work, and the harmony between you, i.e. the training.

Paces

This mark is for your horse's natural gaits and focuses on their freedom and regularity. For a higher mark all three gaits must show correct sequences: if even one gait is less than pure in sequence, the mark cannot be high no matter how good the other two are.

Irregularities in action may come under this heading if the judge believes that there is a genuine problem with the basic gait, such as the start of a subtle lameness; she is not, however, a veterinary surgeon and it is not her job to say that your horse is lame. Irregular steps may also come under impulsion – if your horse pushes unevenly with his two hind legs or stiffens his back so losing elasticity – or submission, when it may be caused by loss of balance or lack of acceptance of the contact.

Impulsion

This heading includes the desire to go forward (an attitude of mind), the energy and elasticity of his movement, the suppleness of his back (a result of relaxation as well as physical suppleness), and the engagement of his hindquarters.

Engagement means that he steps his hind legs well forward underneath his body and does not move them too far backward before he picks them up again to move them forward for the next stride – ideally they should not go very far behind an imaginary perpendicular line drawn to the ground from the point of his buttocks. He should also clearly bend his hind leg joints during the weight-bearing phase of the stride (when his foot is on the ground), so that his hindquarters lower, resulting in a relative raising of his forehand. In other words his hind legs should act rather like springs, coiling down and then thrusting his body upward.

Submission

This includes attention and confidence, harmony, lightness and ease of the movements, acceptance of the bridle and lightness of the forehand.

The main feature characterising submission is willingness: does he understand what you are asking him to do and have enough confidence in you to react without tension? Together with this willingness, the straightness and balance appropriate to the level (if your training has produced this) will present the picture of harmony and lightness that is the ultimate goal of dressage.

Any problems highlighted in this area should cause you to take a good look at the basis of your training, with the emphasis being on developing cooperation and understanding between you, not obedience produced by fear or subordination.

The rider's position and seat

Correctness and effect of the aids – here we come back to the most basic principle of all: your horse will only be able to perform as well as you can ride! To ride with imperceptible aids and to produce an apparently effortless test requires you to develop a truly balanced and supple position, with the toned (but not tense) musculature that allows you to harmonise completely with the movements of your horse, and the education to be able to influence him without impeding him in any way.

Conclusion

Competing Successfully

So, you have managed to organise yourself, your horse, your equipment, and your schedule. You have ridden your tests and studied your sheets. Now the question is: were you successful?

You can measure success against both your original goals and your personal definition of success. You may have achieved everything you set out to do, or you might have fulfilled your goals whilst not making the placings. Possibly you won the class (always pleasing!) whilst not achieving all of the goals that you set for yourself.

Lap of honour with the red rosette.

It is equally possible that things didn't go to plan, and none of your goals was achieved.

All of these outcomes happen in real life; the important thing is to learn from them and to form a strategy for building upon the experience. Looking back at the show, try to identify the following.

- Where you made improvements (even if they were less than you hoped for).

- The areas that need more attention before your next competition.

Probably the most important thing that you can do (along with recognising where you might do things differently another time, or address training issues) is to focus on the good points: improvements, unexpected good behaviour, etc., and to *allow yourself to be pleased with them*. Keep replaying them in your mind to build the positive image that is the firm basis upon which you can take your performances forward – to become a successful dressage competitor.

Index